GCSE RELIGIOUS STUDIES FOR EDEXCEL B

Religion, Philosophy and Social Justice

through Christianity

Gordon Reid and Sarah K Tyler

OXFORD

UNIVERSITY PRESS

OXFORD
UNIVERSITY PRESS

Great Clarendon Street, Oxford, OX2 6DP, United Kingdom

Oxford University Press is a department of the University of Oxford.
It furthers the University's objective of excellence in research,
scholarship, and education by publishing worldwide. Oxford is a
registered trade mark of Oxford University Press in the UK and in
certain other countries

British Library Cataloguing in Publication Data
Data available

978-0-19-837042-0

10 9 8 7 6 5 4 3 2 1

Paper used in the production of this book is a natural, recyclable
product made from wood grown in sustainable forests. The
manufacturing process conforms to the environmental regulations
of the country of origin.

Printed in Great Britain by Bell and Bain Ltd., Glasgow.

Links to third party websites are provided by Oxford in good faith
and for information only. Oxford disclaims any responsibility for the
materials contained in any third party website referenced in this work.

endorsed for
edexcel

In order to ensure that this resource offers high-quality support for
the associated Pearson qualification, it has been through a review
process by the awarding body. This process confirms that this resource
fully covers the teaching and learning content of the specification
or part of a specification at which it is aimed. It also confirms that it
demonstrates an appropriate balance between the development of
subject skills, knowledge and understanding, in addition to preparation
for assessment.

Endorsement does not cover any guidance on assessment activities or
processes (e.g. practice questions or advice on how to answer assessment
questions), included in the resource nor does it prescribe any particular
approach to the teaching or delivery of a related course.

While the publishers have made every attempt to ensure that advice on
the qualification and its assessment is accurate, the official specification
and associated assessment guidance materials are the only authoritative
source of information and should always be referred to for definitive
guidance.

Pearson examiners have not contributed to any sections in this resource
relevant to examination papers for which they have responsibility.

Examiners will not use endorsed resources as a source of material for
any assessment set by Pearson.

Endorsement of a resource does not mean that the resource is required
to achieve this Pearson qualification, nor does it mean that it is the only
suitable material available to support the qualification, and any resource
lists produced by the awarding body shall include this and other
appropriate resources.

Thank you

From the authors:

Our special thanks to Lois and Sarah at OUP – simply brilliant!

From the publisher:

OUP wishes to thank Philip H Robinson, RE Adviser to the CES,
Revd Dr Mark Griffiths, and Elisabeth Hoey for their valuable help
in reviewing and contributing to this book.

Contents

Edexcel GCSE Religious Studies

This book covers all you'll need to study for Edexcel GCSE Religious Studies Paper 3B: Religion, Philosophy and Social Justice through Christianity. Whether you're studying for the full course or the short course, this book will provide the knowledge you'll need, as well as plenty of opportunities to prepare for your GCSE examinations.

GCSE Religious Studies provides the opportunity to study a truly fascinating subject: it will help you to debate big moral issues, understand and analyse a diverse range of opinions, as well as to think for yourself about the meaning of life.

How is the specification covered?

- The Edexcel specification is split into **four sections**:
  - *Christian Beliefs*
  - *Philosophy of Religion*
  - *Living the Christian Life*
  - *Equality*

This book has **four chapters** which match these sections. If you are taking the short course, you will only need to cover the first two sections: *Christian Beliefs*, and *Philosophy of Religion*.

- Each of the four sections of the specification is split into **eight sub-sections**. These cover specific topics, like 'creation', or 'worship'. To support this, each chapter in this book is also split into the same eight sub-sections.

How to use this book

- So that you are fully prepared for your exams, you need to work through every chapter of this book (or just the first two for the short course). At the end of every topic there are exam-style questions which you should use to test your knowledge and practise your writing. Answering exam questions regularly, throughout your GCSE course, will really help you to be confident when exam time arrives.

• In the main topics there are lots of features to guide you through the material:

Specification focus provides you with the relevant description from the Edexcel specification, so that you can see exactly what the exam board expects you to know.

Support features help you to secure important knowledge, and **Stretch** features provide the opportunity for a challenge.

Build your skills are activities that focus on developing the skills you'll need for your exams, and consolidating the knowledge you'll need too.

Sources of wisdom and authority will appear in boxes like this. Important, learnable phrases within a quote will often be in **bold**.

Useful terms are orange in the text and defined here. All of these terms are also provided in an alphabetical **glossary** at the end of the book.

Summary provides a short, bullet-pointed list of key information for ease of reference.

Exam-style questions gives two exam questions so that you can have a go at writing about the information you've studied in that topic. The letter at the start of each question tells you the question type (**a**, **b**, **c**, or **d**), and the number in brackets at the ends tells you how many marks you are aiming for.

• At the end of every chapter there are a few pages called 'Revision and Exam Practice'. These are designed to help you revise the information you have studied in that chapter, and coach you as you practice writing exam answers.

Four **exam-style questions** are provided – one for each of the question types **a**, **b**, **c**, and **d**.

Working through this revision checklist, and following up on anything you might have missed, will help you to make sure you've revised all of the important information from the chapter.

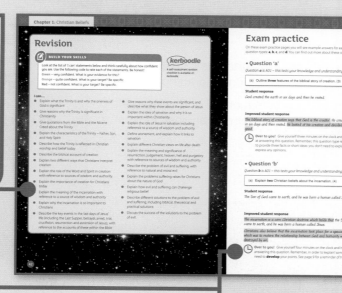

For each exam question, a sample **student answer** is provided, followed by an **improved** version so that you can be guided through improving your own answers.

What went well lists the good things about the first student response. **How to improve** lists its weaknesses, and suggests changes that should be made. These changes are reflected in the 'improved student response'.

Over to you! suggests that you have a go at answering the question yourself under exam conditions, and provides a few final exam tips.

Exam skills: What will the exams be like?

If you are studying the full course, you will sit **two** examinations, each **1 hour and 45 minutes** long. One exam will cover the content in this book (on Christianity), and the other will cover a second faith option.

If you are studying the short course, you will sit **two** examinations, each **50 minutes** long. One exam will cover the first two chapters of content in this book (on Christianity), and the other will cover a second faith option.

You must answer all of the questions on the exam paper.

Exam structure

Because this book covers just **one** of your two exams, the following information relates to that exam. For the full course exam, there will be **four questions** to answer. For the short course exam, there will be **two questions** to answer. Each question will relate to one of the four chapters in this book:

1. **Christian Beliefs**
2. **Philosophy of Religion**
3. **Living the Christian Life**
4. **Equality**

Short course: answer two questions on these first two topics

Full course: answer four questions, one for each of these four topics

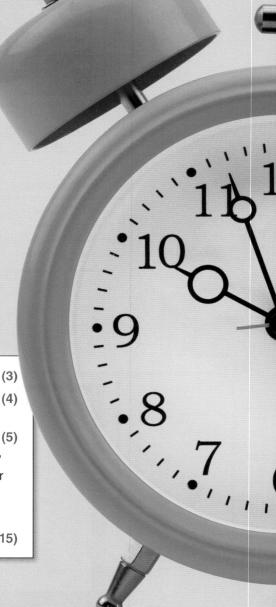

Each question will be split into four parts: **a**, **b**, **c**, and **d**. For example, your first question on the exam (covering *1. Christian Beliefs*) could be something like this:

---

1   (a)   Outline **three** features of the Trinity.   (3)

      (b)   Explain **two** types of evil.   (4)

      (c)   Explain **two** reasons why the resurrection is important to Christians. In your answer you must refer to a source of wisdom and authority.   (5)

      (d)   "Christianity provides no solutions to the problem of evil and suffering." Evaluate this statement considering arguments for and against. In your response you should:
- refer to Christian teachings
- refer to different Christian points of view
- reach a justified conclusion.   (15)

The 'a' question

The 'a' question will always start with the words 'Outline **three**…' or 'State **three**', and the maximum number of marks awarded will be three marks. For example:

> **1** (a) Outline **three** features of the Trinity. **(3)**

The 'b' question

The 'b' question will always start with the words 'Explain **two**…' or 'Describe **two**…', and the maximum number of marks awarded will be four marks. For example:

> (b) Explain **two** types of evil. **(4)**

The 'c' question

The 'c' question will always start with the words 'Explain **two**…', and will ask you to refer to a source of wisdom and authority. The maximum number of marks awarded will be five marks. For example:

> (c) Explain **two** reasons why the resurrection is important to Christians.
> In your answer you must refer to a source of wisdom and authority. **(5)**

The 'd' question

The 'd' question will always start with a statement of opinion that you are asked to evaluate. These questions will sometimes be out of 12 marks, and sometimes be out of 15 marks (see page 11, 'Written communication', to find out why!). For example:

> (d) "Christianity provides no solutions to the problem of evil and suffering."
> Evaluate this statement considering arguments for and against. In your response you should:
> - refer to Christian teachings
> - refer to different Christian points of view
> - reach a justified conclusion. **(15)**

Know your question types!

…that way, nothing in your exam will take you by surprise!

Exam skills: How will the exams be marked?

When you're revising and practising using exam questions, it will really help you to understand how you'll be marked. If you know what the examiners are looking for, then you're more likely to do well!

Assessment Objectives

Examiners will mark your work using two Assessment Objectives: Assessment Objective 1 (AO1), and Assessment Objective 2 (AO2). The two Assessment Objectives are described in the table below.

	Students must:	Weighting
AO1	Demonstrate knowledge and understanding of religion and belief, including: <ul><li>beliefs, practices and sources of authority</li><li>influence on individuals, communities and societies</li><li>similarities and differences within and/or between religions and beliefs.</li></ul>	50%
AO2	Analyse and evaluate aspects of religion and belief, including their significance and influence.	50%

You need to remember that 50% of the marks available in your exam will be awarded for demonstrating **knowledge and understanding of religion and belief** (AO1), and 50% of the marks available will be awarded for **analysing and evaluating aspects of religion and belief** (AO2).

Marking the 'a' question

'Outline/State' questions are assessed using Assessment Objective 1 (knowledge) only. These questions require you to provide three facts or short ideas: **you don't need to explain them or express any opinions**. For example, in answer to the question 'Outline **three** features of the Trinity', your three responses could be:

1. There is one God in three persons (1)

2. Each person is fully God (1)

3. Each person is different from the other persons (1)

For each response, you would receive 1 mark. You're not expected to spend time explaining what the Trinity is: the question only asks you to give three features.

Marking the 'b' question

Like the 'a' question, 'b' questions are assessed using Assessment Objective 1 (knowledge) only. However, 'b' questions start with 'Explain' or 'Describe', which means you will need to show **development** of ideas. For example, if the question is 'Explain **two** types of evil' you might think you just need to state the two types, but this means you can only be awarded **a maximum of two marks**:

Type 1: One type of evil is called natural evil (1)

Type 2: Another type of evil is called moral evil (1)

The types given above are correct, but the student would only score 2 marks out of 4. In order to fully **explain** these reasons, you need to show some **development**. For example:

Type 1: One type of evil is called natural evil (1), **which means evil caused by nature, e.g. earthquakes (1)**

Type 2: Another type of evil is called moral evil (1), **which means evil caused by humans, e.g. murder (1)**

Each of the above points are now developed, and would receive 2 marks each, totalling **4 marks**.

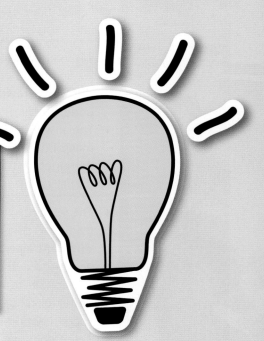

CONNECTIVES

A **connective** helps you to develop your basic answer. There are lots of different types of connective (therefore/because/and/consequently/a result of this is/this means that). However, take care not to simply repeat the question and then use a connective, as that is not a developed answer and is only worth one mark. For example, 'Christians believe in two types of evil, **and** one of these is called natural evil' would only receive one mark despite the use of a connective.

Marking the 'c' question

Like the 'a' and 'b' questions, 'c' questions are assessed using Assessment Objective 1 (knowledge) only. 'C' questions are very similar to 'b' questions (they begin with 'Explain **two**' and require two developed points), but they have one crucial difference. For an extra mark, you are expected to include a reference to a **source of wisdom and authority**, which could be a quotation from/reference to the Bible or another important source within Christianity. For example, here's a student answer to a five mark question:

(c) Explain **two** reasons why the resurrection is important to Christians. In your answer you must refer to a source of wisdom and authority. **(5)**

Christians believe that Jesus' resurrection allows their sins to be forgiven **(1)**. Therefore, they can have a true relationship with God again **(1)**. If Christians repent, they will be forgiven (Luke 24: 47) **(1)**.

Jesus' resurrection means that death is not the end **(1)**; this means that he showed that death could be overcome and he paved the way for Christians to be with God **(1)**.

You need to write **two** developed points, one of which needs to be supported by a source of wisdom and authority. Setting out your writing in two paragraphs makes it clear that it is two developed points. You could directly quote a source, or you could just include the reference (as in the above student answer).

Marking the 'd' question

The 'd' question is marked using AO2 (analysis/evaluation). These questions specifically ask you to evaluate a statement. Evaluating a statement means that you are weighing up how good or true it is. The best way to evaluate something is to consider different opinions on the matter – and this is exactly what the question asks you to do. When you are planning your answer, you need to remember to do the following:

- Refer to Christian teachings – for instance core beliefs and important sources of wisdom and authority

- Ensure that different viewpoints are included either from within Christianity or non-religious views, and ensure that relevant ethical or philosophical arguments are referred to (the question will make it clear which of these will be required in your answer)

- Ensure that you include a justified conclusion – in other words, your final decision on the matter having considered different viewpoints.

If you don't refer to different viewpoints, **you cannot get more than half of the marks**.

The examiner will mark your answer using a **mark scheme**, similar to the one below.

Level 1 (1–3 marks)	• Basic information or reasons about the issue are identified and can be explained by some religious or moral understanding. • Opinions are given but not fully explained.
Level 2 (4–6 marks)	• Some information or reasons about the issue are loosely identified and can be explained by limited religious or moral understanding. • Opinions are given which attempt to support the issue but are not fully explained or justified.
Level 3 (7–9 marks)	• Information given clearly describes religious information/issues, leading to coherent and logical chains of reasoning **that consider different viewpoints**. These are supported by an accurate understanding of religion and belief. • The answer contains coherent and reasoned judgements of many, but not all, of the elements in the question. Judgements are supported by a good understanding of evidence, leading to a partially justified conclusion.
Level 4 (10–12 marks)	• The response critically deconstructs religious information/issues, leading to coherent and logical chains of reasoning **that consider different viewpoints.** These are supported by a sustained, accurate and thorough understanding of religion and belief. • The answer contains coherent and reasoned judgements of the full range of elements in the question. Judgements are fully supported by the comprehensive use of evidence, leading to a fully justified conclusion.

ARE YOU READY?

Written communication

Some of the marks in your exam will be awarded purely for the quality of your 'written communication'. Written communication includes your use of correct **spelling, punctuation and grammar**, as well as the use of **specialist terminology**.

These marks will be awarded in questions **1(d)** and **3(d)**: These are the long essay questions on topics 1 and 3 (*Christian Beliefs and Living the Christian Life*). Whereas 'd' questions in topics 2 and 4 are out of 12 marks, these will be out of **15 marks**, and the extra 3 marks in each question are awarded solely for your written communication. You'll know which questions these are in the exam because they will be shown with an asterisk (*) and have a really clear instruction above them:

> **In this question, 3 of the marks awarded will be for your spelling, punctuation and grammar and your use of specialist terminology.**
>
> *(d) "Christianity provides no solutions to the problem of evil and suffering."
>
> Evaluate this statement considering arguments for and against. In your response you should:
> * refer to Christian teachings
> * refer to different Christian points of view
> * reach a justified conclusion. **(15)**

In these questions:

* 0 marks are awarded if there are considerable errors or irrelevant information
* 1 mark is awarded for reasonable accuracy and limited use of religious terms
* 2 marks are awarded for considerable accuracy and a good number of specialist terms
* 3 marks are awarded for consistent accuracy and a wide range of specialist terms.

Good written communication is always important, but you will only receive marks for it in questions **1(d)** and **3(d)**. Therefore, you should allow yourself time in your exam to check these two essays carefully and amend any errors.

Introduction to Christianity

What is Christianity?

Christianity is the main religious tradition in Great Britain. Other religious traditions include Islam, Buddhism, Judaism, Hinduism and Sikhism.

Central to Christianity is a man named Jesus, whose existence in 1st century Palestine has been recorded by early Roman and Jewish scholars. The life and impact of Jesus is described in the New Testament of the Bible – the Christian holy book – including the claim that Jesus is the Son of God, and accounts of the work of his followers, the early Christians.

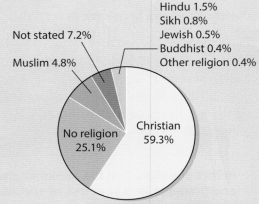

Hindu 1.5%
Sikh 0.8%
Jewish 0.5%
Buddhist 0.4%
Other religion 0.4%
Not stated 7.2%
Muslim 4.8%
No religion 25.1%
Christian 59.3%

The 2011 England and Wales census asked people, 'What is your religion?'. This pie chart shows how people responded.

What do Christians believe?

Christians believe in one God in three persons: God the Father, God the Son (who came to earth as Jesus) and God the Holy Spirit (see 1.1). Christians believe that God loves them, and wants to have a relationship with them. They believe that, because of this love, he sent Jesus to live amongst them, to die on a cross and be raised to life three days later. They believe he did this to free humanity from sin, and make it possible for them to spend eternity with God in heaven (see 1.3–1.5).

While he was on earth, Jesus chose twelve specific followers, who are known within Christianity as the apostles, or disciples. He also had many other followers however, including women and children. According to the Bible, after his death and resurrection Jesus' followers gathered in Jerusalem, and the number of followers grew quickly from hundreds to thousands as the apostles began to teach about Jesus and the things they had experienced.

What are the different groups within Christianity?

Today, Christianity has followers all over the world. The word 'denomination' is used to describe a particular group within Christianity. There are many different denominations which you will learn about in this book.

The Catholic Church and the Orthodox Church

The Catholic Church was the only Christian Church until 1054CE. Around 1054CE, a new denomination was formed, one that we now refer to as the Orthodox Church. There were many reasons why this split occurred, but a key reason was that the Orthodox Church did not believe the Pope should have ultimate authority.

The Protestant denominations

In 1517, Martin Luther, a Catholic Priest, challenged a range of Catholic practices. His followers were called 'Lutherans', and shortly after, the Lutheran Church was formed. It was, in effect, the first of the Protestant denominations, which developed as a 'protest' against the practices of the Catholic Church.

Since that time, a number of Protestant denominations have formed, for example:

- The Church of England (sometimes called the Anglican Church)
- The Baptist Church
- The Methodist Church
- The Salvation Army
- Pentecostal denominations.

New denominations continue to form today, and usually come out of existing denominations. They are formed because of differences over two main factors:

1. Governance (the way the denomination is structured)
2. Theology (what the denomination believes).

Today, it is very important to understand that there is a lot of overlap between denominations, particularly the larger denominations. For example, charismatic worship (traditionally associated with the Pentecostal church) can be found in Anglican and Catholic churches (see 3.1). Many churches also work together, which is called ecumenism (see 3.7).

Christians in Great Britain today

From a dozen people in Jerusalem in the 1st century, Christianity now has more than 2.4 billion believers all over the world. In Great Britain, Christianity is still the main religious tradition, despite a growing number of people who do not identify with any particular religion.

The study of Christianity will enable you to develop a greater understanding of the practice of Christianity in Great Britain and the wider world, and to consider the values held by Christians. This book provides you with opportunities to make your own observations, raise questions, and draw personal conclusions about various teachings, beliefs and important issues.

Chapter 1: Christian Beliefs

1.1 The Trinity

What is the Trinity?

The **Trinity** is unique to Christianity. It is the belief that there is only one God, but that he exists in three 'persons':

● God the Father

● God the Son

● God the Holy Spirit (sometimes called the Holy Ghost).

Each of these three persons is fully God, but they are not *three* Gods – they are *one* God.

The Nicene Creed

The Nicene Creed is a statement of belief that many Christians recite in church. It says of the Trinity:

> ❝We believe in one God, the Father, the Almighty, maker of heaven and earth [...] We believe in one Lord, **Jesus Christ**, the only Son of God, eternally **begotten** of the Father [...] We believe in the **Holy Spirit**, the giver of life, who proceeds from the Father and the Son.❞

The Nicene Creed reveals the following about the nature of the Trinity:

● **God the Father** is the creator of the universe and is the 'Almighty' (having complete power).

● **God the Son** is Jesus Christ who is 'Lord' and the Son of the Father.

● **God the Holy Spirit** comes from the Father and the Son. Christians believe the Holy Spirit is the 'giver of life', meaning he is spiritually active in the world, he helps them to know God and worship him, and he equips and empowers believers.

What is the 'oneness' of God?

The Trinity can be a difficult idea to understand. For example, how can God be 'one' and 'three' at the same time? Think of the Trinity like diagram **A**. There is one God. There are three different persons, each of whom is different to the other two but each of whom is fully God. This is the special 'oneness' of God.

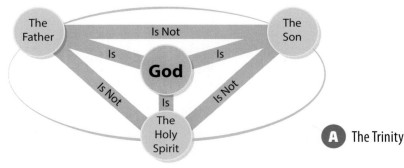

A The Trinity

This quotation contains some difficult ideas: **SUPPORT**

● '**eternally begotten**' means that the Son of God has always existed, and is in a relationship as Son of the Father.

● '**proceeds from the Father**' means the Holy Spirit comes directly (proceeds) from God. Like the Son of God, the Holy Spirit is not *made by* God but *is* God.

 USEFUL TERMS

Begotten: born of

Holy Spirit: the Spirit of God, which gives the power to understand and worship

Jesus Christ: the Son of God, who came into the world as a human being

Trinity: God as one being, in three persons

The persons of the Trinity

The word 'Trinity' does not appear in the Bible. However, there is one event, described in the Gospel of Matthew, where the persons of the Trinity do all appear together. This is when Jesus is baptised before beginning his ministry in the world:

> 'As soon as **Jesus** was baptised, he went up out of the water. At that moment heaven was opened, and he saw **the Spirit of God** descending like a dove and alighting on him. And a **voice from heaven** said, "This is my Son, whom I love; with him I am well pleased." '
> *(Matthew 3: 16–17)*

This is important because it shows the Trinity working together as one – Jesus is baptised to begin his ministry, the Father speaks his approval, and the Holy Spirit, with the power of the Father, enables Jesus to begin his work.

B *The Baptism of Christ*, a painting by Paolo Veronese (c.1580CE–1588CE)

STRETCH

Look at this painting and the corresponding story in the Bible (*Matthew 3: 13–17*). Can you find three different symbolic ideas? Why do you think these ideas are important for Christians?

> 'Therefore go and make disciples of all nations, baptising them in the name of the Father and of the Son and of the Holy Spirit. '
> *(Matthew 28: 19)*

> 'The grace of our Lord Jesus Christ, and the love of God, and the fellowship of the Holy Spirit be with you. '
> *(2 Corinthians 13: 14)*

The Bible highlights the importance of each person of the Trinity and how they can be understood and worshipped by Christians today.

How is the Trinity reflected in worship and belief today?

Christians use the Trinity as the guide for worship and belief. Christians believe that the Trinity displays God's loving nature, which impacts on their worship.

- **God the Father:** Christians believe that God the Father, as the creator, cares for all that he has made. They pray to him in the knowledge that he cares about them and is powerful, like Jesus did in the Lord's Prayer: 'This, then, is how you should pray: "Our Father in heaven, hallowed be your name …"' *(Matthew 6: 9)*.

- **God the Son:** Christians believe that, around 5BCE, God the Son became a human being (see 1.3), and he was given the name Jesus. Christians believe Jesus is their saviour, friend and role-model. They follow the example set by Jesus, who came into the world to teach people how to live lives of goodness, love and faith. A core belief about Jesus is that he died to take the punishment for the sins of **humanity** (see 1.5). Worship is therefore often happy and joyful, as Christians express their thanks to God for forgiving their sins and to Jesus for the sacrifice he made.

- **God the Holy Spirit:** Christians believe that the Holy Spirit is their comforter and guide. They believe that the Holy Spirit lives in their hearts and not only enables them to lead good lives and make the right moral choices, but also helps them to praise and worship God. **Charismatic** churches, such as the Pentecostal Church and an increasing number of Anglican churches, will ask the Holy Spirit to enable them to worship using **spiritual gifts**. These church services are often less formal and involve dancing and creative expression.

USEFUL TERMS

Charismatic: a power given by God, e.g. inspired teaching

Humanity: all human beings

Spiritual gifts: gifts given by God to believers, e.g. speaking in 'tongues', a special language

C A church meeting that involves charismatic worship. Can you identify any special features of this kind of worship?

Christians believe that the Trinity is a model of mutual love and perfect unity. It helps Christians to understand more about relationships because the Trinity is very similar to the way they live. They are not alone, they have families and friends who they can talk to, enjoy time with, and often love. In the same way, Christians believe the Trinity is a loving relationship with each of the three persons relating to the others – just like a family. This 'oneness' is reflected in Christian songs and hymns:

> ❛Shine, Jesus, shine, fill this land with the Father's glory. Blaze, Spirit, blaze, set our hearts on fire.❜
> *'Shine, Jesus, Shine', by Graham Kendrick*

> ❛Holy, holy, holy, Lord God Almighty […] God in three persons, blessed Trinity!❜
> *'Holy, Holy, Holy', by Reginald Heber*

Christians are baptised 'in the name of the Father and of the Son and of the Holy Spirit' (*Matthew 28: 19*) (see 3.2) and sometimes the sign of the cross is made with a hand gesture in three movements, reflecting the Trinity.

BUILD YOUR SKILLS

1   In pairs, write down in your own words how you would describe the Trinity. As you do so, consider the following aspects:
   - How can God be 'one' and 'three' at the same time?
   - How are the three persons different from each other?
   - Do you think the idea of the Trinity makes God easier or harder to understand? Why?

2   a   What are the reasons why Christians feel that they should believe in the Trinity?
   b   How does the idea of the Trinity help Christians?

3   Look at image **D**. How would the Holy Spirit enable Christians to respond in this situation?

EXAM-STYLE QUESTIONS

b   Explain **two** Christian beliefs about the Trinity. (4)

c   Explain **two** reasons why the concept of the Trinity is important for Christians. In your answer you must refer to a source of wisdom and authority. (5)

SUMMARY

- Christians believe in the concept of the Trinity. God is one, God is in three persons (Father, Son and Holy Spirit), and each person is fully God.

- In the Bible, all three persons were present at the baptism of Jesus (*Matthew 3: 13–17*).

- Christians worship God the Father and Jesus Christ in a formal way or in private, and many believe that the Holy Spirit helps them to worship in the most fulfilling way.

D

1.2 Creation

What is the biblical account of creation?

There are two accounts of creation in Genesis, the first book of the Bible. The first, in *Genesis 1:1–2:3*, contains the story of the creation of the earth by God in six days. God speaks and things happen:

SPECIFICATION FOCUS

The creation of the universe and of humanity: the biblical account of creation and divergent ways in which it may be understood by Christians including as literal and metaphorical; the role of the Word and Spirit in creation including John 1: 1–18 and Genesis 1–3; the importance of creation for Christians today.

Day 1 Heavens, earth, light and dark
Day 2 Water and sky
Day 3 Land and plant life
Day 4 Sun, moon, and stars
Day 5 Fish and birds
Day 6 Land animals and humans

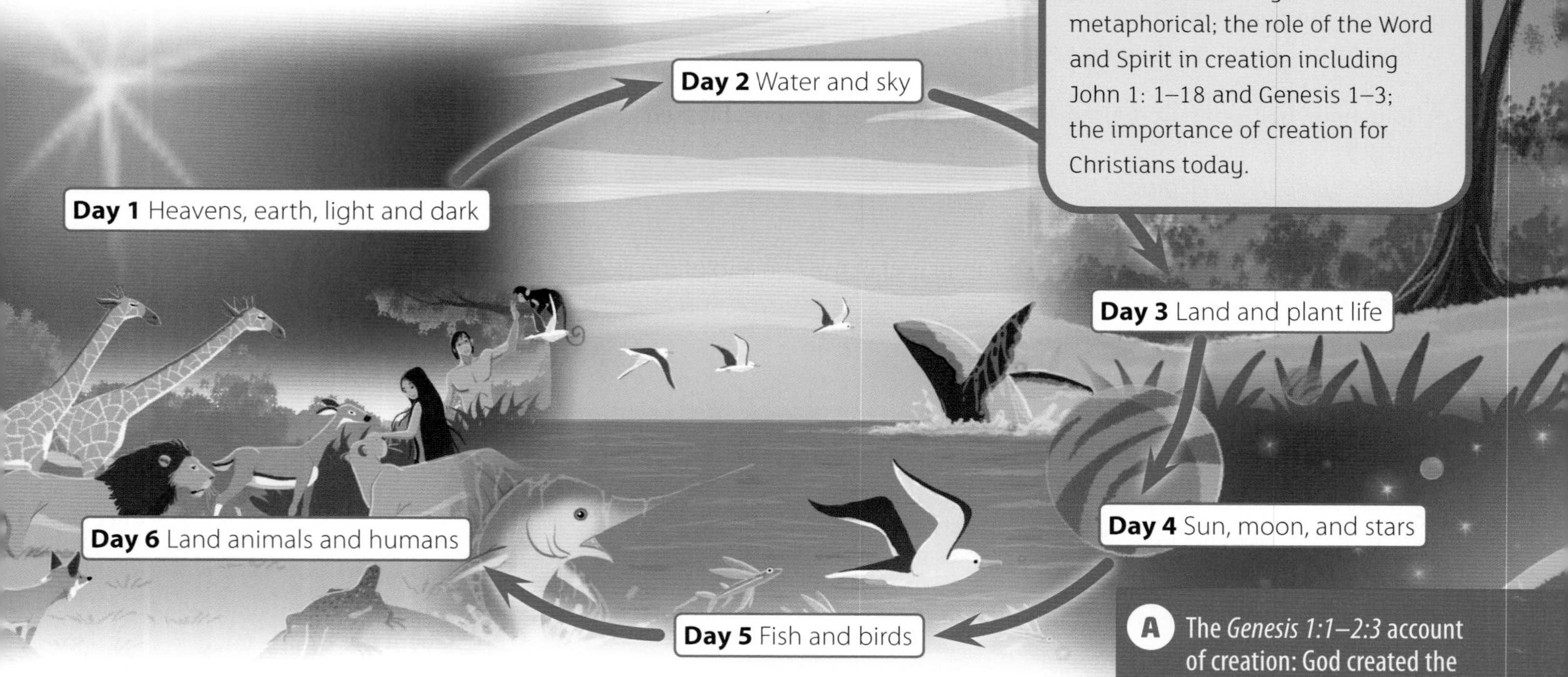

A The *Genesis 1:1–2:3* account of creation: God created the earth in six days and rested on the seventh day

The second account, in *Genesis 2:4–3:23*, is different because it concentrates on the development of humans:

1. ‘Then **the Lord God formed a man** from the dust of the ground and breathed into his nostrils the breath of life, and the man became a living being.’ *(Genesis 2: 7)*

2. ‘The Lord God took the man and placed him in **the Garden of Eden** to work it and take care of it.’ *(Genesis 2: 15)*

3. ‘And the Lord God commanded the man, “You are free to eat from any tree in the garden; but **you must not eat from the tree of the knowledge of good and evil**, for when you eat from it you will certainly die.”’ *(Genesis 2: 16–17)*

4. ‘Then **the Lord God made a woman** from the rib he had taken out of the man...’ *(Genesis 2: 22)*

5. ‘When the woman saw that the fruit of the tree was good [...] **she took some and ate it. She also gave some to her husband...**’ *(Genesis 3: 6–7)*

6. ‘So the Lord God banished him from the Garden of Eden...’ *(Genesis 3: 23)*

How can the biblical account of creation be understood in different ways?

There are differing views on exactly what the Bible means in the accounts of creation:

- **The metaphorical view:** Many Christians believe this account is a metaphor, and is not literally true. They would argue that it is a story to help people to understand that God is the creator of all things.

- **The literal view:** Others believe that the Bible account is literally true and God created the world exactly as the Bible says. This is called **creationism**. Creationists believe that the Bible is the sacred word of God and believe that it should be interpreted literally where possible. Young Earth Creationists believe that the world was made in six days approximately 10,000 years ago.

USEFUL TERMS

Creationism: the belief that the world was created in a literal six days and that Genesis is a scientific/historical account of the beginning of the world

What is the role of the Word and Spirit?

The Bible teaches that God the Father, Son and Holy Spirit – the Trinity – were all involved in the act of creation.

The Word

In the New Testament, the Gospel of John says:

> ❛**In the beginning was the Word**, and the Word was with God, and the Word was God.❜
> *(John 1:1)*

> ❛**Through him** [the Word] **all things were made** [...] In him was life...❜
> *(John 1: 3–4)*

STRETCH

Read the full quotation in *John 1: 1–18*. Can you explain how this passage links to the ideas of **incarnation** and **salvation**? (See 1.3 and 1.5).

But who is the 'Word'? The answer is Jesus, because the Gospel goes on to say, 'The Word became flesh and made his dwelling among us…' (*John 1: 14*). So Christians believe that God the Son (Jesus) was with God the Father at the start, acting in the creation. They believe he is the source of life.

The Book of Genesis also says that God created not by using his hands, but by speaking: 'God said…' (*Genesis 1: 3*). Of course, what he speaks are words – hence Jesus is 'the Word'. As it says in the Book of Psalms, 'By the word of the Lord were the heavens made…' (*Psalm 33: 6*).

The Spirit

In the Book of Genesis it says that during the act of creation the 'Spirit of God was hovering over the waters' (*Genesis 1: 2*). This image describes the Holy Spirit as present in creation to protect what has, and will be, created. The Spirit (Hebrew: 'breath') of God guards creation.

Why is creation important for Christians today?

The relationship between humans and their creator

The Bible says that man and woman were created in the image of God. Christians therefore believe that human beings are important to God, as he expressed something of himself in creating them.

- At the start, when God creates man and woman (Adam and Eve), they walk and talk with God in a relationship of love and devotion. God said, 'I give you every seed-bearing plant […] and every tree' (*Genesis 1: 29*).
- God gave Adam and Eve **free will**, but they chose to disobey God by eating from the forbidden tree. The relationship of mutual love and trust between God and humanity was broken.
- God therefore sent Adam and Eve out of the Garden of Eden and ordered them to work the ground: 'By the sweat of your brow you will eat your food […] for dust you are and to dust you will return' (*Genesis 3: 19*).
- Today, Christians believe that they have a personal and loving relationship with God and that they can pray to God for guidance. They believe that God has given humanity the opportunity to care for creation, with God's guidance and help.

The relationship between humans and the rest of creation

Christians believe that:

- God gave humans the responsibility to look after the world as his 'stewards' (in *Genesis 1: 26*). This means that they are to have authority over the animals, plants and other resources.
- God blessed humans and said, 'Be fruitful and increase in number; fill the earth and subdue it. Rule over the fish in the sea and the birds in the sky and over every living creature that moves on the ground.' (*Genesis 1: 28*).
- They should care for the environment so that the world can be passed on to future generations as a better place than when they found it. This is called **stewardship**.

Christians believe humans should:

- treat animals and the land kindly
- leave the world better than they found it
- share things fairly
- be judged by God on their actions.

This means humans should take on certain duties:

- reduction of pollution
- **conservation** of resources
- sharing with the poor
- conservation of the **environment**.

> **USEFUL TERMS**
>
> **Conservation:** protecting something from being damaged or destroyed
>
> **Environment:** the surroundings in which plants and animals live and on which they depend for life
>
> **Free will:** having the freedom to choose what to do
>
> **Stewardship:** looking after something so it can be passed on to the next generation

> **STRETCH**
>
> Interestingly, at the time of Jesus, the people of Israel would celebrate a 'Year of Jubilee', when no crops were planted, to give the land a well-earned rest: 'The fiftieth year shall be a jubilee for you; do not sow and do not reap' (*Leviticus 25: 11*). Is this a good idea? Why/why not?

BUILD YOUR SKILLS

1   Copy and complete the following table for the main ideas about creation given in this unit. Three ideas have been suggested for you. **SUPPORT**

Term/idea	What does it mean?	Why is it important for Christians?
Creation		
Stewardship		
Made in the image of God		

2   Which aspects of the biblical account of creation are **a** most convincing and **b** least convincing? Why?

3   Is God's punishment of Adam and Eve fair and just? Why/why not?

4   Look at this car used by campaigners, in image **C**.
   a   What is the message being conveyed? Is it pro-creationist or anti-creationist?
   b   Make a list of arguments that support creationism and a list of arguments against. Which are the most convincing arguments, and why?

5   What comes first, stopping pollution or fulfilling human needs? For example, is it right to shut down a polluting factory if it means 1000 people will lose their jobs? **STRETCH**

SUMMARY

- There are two accounts of how God created the world and humanity in the book of Genesis, and there is another account in *John 1: 1–18*.

- Some Christians believe these accounts are literally true, whilst others think they are metaphorical.

- Christians believe that God has made them stewards, with a duty to care for the world and its resources.

EXAM-STYLE QUESTIONS

a   Outline **three** Christian beliefs about creation. (3)

d   'A Christian should believe the world was made in seven days.' Evaluate this statement considering arguments for and against. In your response you should:
   • refer to Christian teachings
   • refer to different Christian points of view
   • reach a justified conclusion. (15)

1.3 The incarnation

What is the incarnation?

Christians believe that Jesus Christ is the Son of God, who came down to earth to live as a man from around 5BCE to around 33CE. This is called the **incarnation**. You will be learning about the life and significance of Jesus in 1.3–1.5.

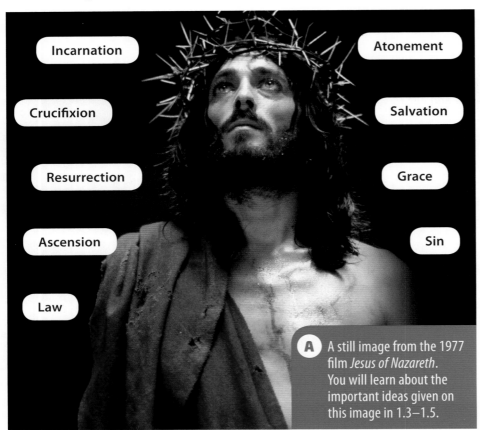

Incarnation

Atonement

Crucifixion

Salvation

Resurrection

Grace

Ascension

Sin

Law

A A still image from the 1977 film *Jesus of Nazareth*. You will learn about the important ideas given on this image in 1.3–1.5.

How is the incarnation shown in the Bible?

For Christians, God the Son, the second person of the Trinity, became a human being in Jesus of Nazareth. The Bible describes the incarnation in this way:

> ❛The virgin will conceive and give birth to a son, and **they will call him Immanuel**.❜
> *(Matthew 1: 23)*

> ❛The Word became flesh and made his dwelling among us.❜
> *(John 1: 14)*

The Bible teaches that God the Son came into the world to live among people, show them what God was like and enable them to have a relationship with him.

The Bible also describes the incarnation as a great mystery, because there are aspects of it that are amazing and beyond human understanding:

> ❛Beyond all question, **the mystery from which true godliness springs is great**: He appeared in the flesh, was vindicated by the Spirit, was seen by angels, was preached among the nations, was believed on in the world, was taken up in glory.❜
> *(1 Timothy 3: 16)*

STRETCH What aspects of the incarnation are mysterious and why? Refer to this quotation from 1 Timothy in your answer.

SUPPORT **Vindicated** means proven to be true or genuine.

What is the importance of the incarnation for Christians today?

- Christians believe that Jesus is God incarnate. They believe Jesus came into the world to enable the relationship between God and humanity to be restored (see 1.2). The incarnation is therefore important for Christians because it allows them to have a relationship with God.

- Christians believe that the incarnation shows that God loves the world and the people in it. This is what they celebrate during Christmas (see 3.5). Christians celebrate the incarnation on Christmas Day by singing Christmas carols and remembering the story of the birth of Jesus.

- Christians believe that, as a human, Jesus could understand humanity and its problems, and identify with their suffering.

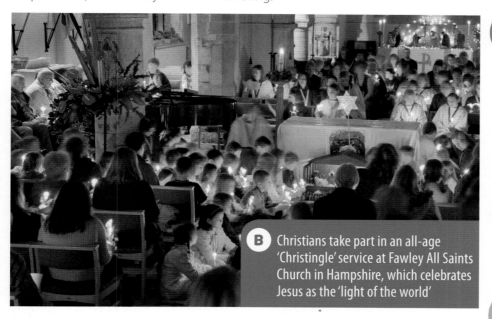

B Christians take part in an all-age 'Christingle' service at Fawley All Saints Church in Hampshire, which celebrates Jesus as the 'light of the world'

BUILD YOUR SKILLS

1   a   With a partner or in a small group, write down a list of reasons why the incarnation might be true, and a list for why it might be false.
    b   Which are the strongest reasons and why?

2   Why is the incarnation important for Christians? Explain two reasons in your own words. Refer to a source of wisdom and authority.

? EXAM-STYLE QUESTIONS

a   Outline **three** Christian beliefs about Jesus. (3)
c   Explain **two** Christian beliefs about the incarnation of Jesus. In your answer you must refer to a source of wisdom and authority. (5)

SUMMARY

- Christians believe that God came into the world as Jesus, a man. This is called the incarnation.

- The purpose of the incarnation was to enable human beings to have a relationship with God.

1.4 The last days of Jesus' life

What happened in the last days of Jesus' life and why are these events important?

The Last Supper and betrayal

The evening before he died, Jesus and his disciples had a meal together, which Christians call the Last Supper. At the meal, Jesus spoke about his forthcoming death. He tried to prepare the disciples for the future by teaching them to serve one another *(Luke 22: 26–27)*. He explained that after he was gone he would send the Holy Spirit to 'teach you all things and remind you of everything I have said to you' *(John 14: 26)*.

Jesus also gave the disciples bread to eat and wine to drink. He said that they are his 'body' and his 'blood'. They represented his sacrifice –'This is my body given for you' *(Luke 22: 19)* (see 3.2).

Jesus also knew that one of the disciples would betray him, having him arrested by the Jewish authorities. He said to the disciples: 'the hand of him who is going to betray me is with mine on the table. […] But woe to that man who betrays [me]' *(Luke 22: 21–22)*. It was Judas Iscariot who betrayed him.

For Christians, these events highlight that Jesus' teachings had begun to come true – he knew what was going to happen. Christians remember the Last Supper when they take part in the Eucharist (see 3.2).

SPECIFICATION FOCUS

The last days of Jesus' life: the Last Supper, betrayal, arrest, trial, crucifixion, resurrection and ascension of Jesus; the accounts of these within the Bible including Luke 22–24 and the significance of these events to understanding the person of Jesus Christ.

> **STRETCH**
> Read the full story in Luke 22: 7–38. What can Christians learn about the person of Jesus from this passage?

A *The Sacrament of the Last Supper* by Salvador Dalí (1955)

Jesus' betrayal, arrest, and trial

Jesus and the disciples planned to spend the night in a garden called Gethsemane. In the middle of the night, Judas Iscariot brought an armed crowd to take Jesus away. Judas identified Jesus to the authorities by kissing him *(Luke 22: 47–48)*.

Jesus was taken before the Jewish High Council, called the Sanhedrin. They found Jesus guilty of blasphemy for claiming to be the Son of God. They believed that this was a great crime which should be punished by death.

After this, the Jewish leaders took Jesus to the Roman governor, Pontius Pilate, who sentenced Jesus to death even though Pilate thought he was innocent: "'Why? What crime has this man committed? I have found in him no grounds for the death penalty'" *(Luke 23: 22)*.

Blasphemy means insulting or showing a lack of respect for God.

SUPPORT

The crucifixion

Jesus was put to death by **crucifixion**, which means being nailed to a cross and left to die. He was crucified between two criminals. The sky went dark from midday until around 3pm, when he died.

> ❛Wanting to release Jesus, Pilate appealed to them again. But they kept shouting, **"Crucify him! Crucify him!"**❜
> *(Luke 23: 20–21)*

> ❛It was now about noon, and darkness came over the whole land until three in the afternoon, for the sun stopped shining. And the curtain of the temple was torn in two. Jesus called out with a loud voice, "Father, into your hands I commit my spirit." When he had said this, he breathed his last. The centurion, seeing what had happened, praised God and said, "Surely this was a righteous man."❜
> *(Luke 23: 44–47)*

For Christians, Jesus' death on the cross was proof of his humanity – he did actually die. This means that Jesus truly was God incarnate.

Christians believe Jesus' death was a sacrifice – his death brought about the forgiveness of humanity's **sins**. Through Jesus' death and resurrection, forgiveness becomes available to humanity and the loving relationship with God is restored (see 1.5).

Christians remember the crucifixion on Good Friday through worship, hymn-singing and prayers.

USEFUL TERMS

Crucifixion: being nailed to a cross and left to die

Sin: anything that prevents a relationship with God, either because the person does something they shouldn't, or neglects to do something they should

B An image from the 2004 film *The Passion of the Christ*, showing Jesus carrying the cross on which he is to be crucified

USEFUL TERMS

Ascension: going up into heaven

Resurrection: rising from the dead

Jesus' resurrection

The Bible teaches that Jesus rose from the dead on the third day after he died. This is called the **resurrection**. For Christians, it shows that Jesus really was God and could overcome death.

A group of women went to Jesus' tomb to prepare his body for a proper burial. They discovered that the body had gone. According to the Bible, Jesus had risen:

> ❝Why do you look for the living among the dead? **He is not here; he has risen!** Remember how he told you [...] The Son of Man must be delivered over to the hands of sinners, be crucified and on the third day be raised again.❞
> *(Luke 24: 5–7)*

For Christians, this is important because it means that all Jesus taught is true. It means that humanity's sins are forgiven, people can have a true relationship with God again, and death is no longer the end. Christians believe that, if they believe in Jesus and follow his teachings, they will receive eternal life and be reunited with God. They remember the resurrection on Easter Sunday, which is a joyful celebration.

> ❝... you, with the help of wicked men, put him to death by nailing him to the cross. But **God raised him from the dead**, freeing him from the agony of death, because it was impossible for death to keep its hold on him.❞
> *(Acts 2: 23–24)*

> ❝**Christ died for our sins** according to the scriptures, that he was buried, that he was raised on the third day...❞
> *(1 Corinthians 15: 3–4)*

C According to the Bible, Jesus' tomb was found to be empty, with the large stone door rolled to one side

What does it mean to say that Jesus overcame death? Did Jesus die and then rise from the dead? Give reasons for your point of view. If Jesus didn't die, what do you think did happen? **STRETCH**

Jesus' ascension

The Bible teaches that, after Jesus rose from the dead, he spent time teaching his disciples. He told them that he would soon be taken up to heaven but that they would not be left alone. The Holy Spirit would come into the world and help them to spread the word of God.

> "… in a few days you will be baptised with the Holy Spirit. […] You will receive power when the Holy Spirit comes on you; and you will be my witnesses in Jerusalem, and in all Judea and Samaria, and to the ends of the earth." After he said this, **he was taken up before their very eyes**, and a cloud hid him from their sight.
> *(Acts 1: 5–9)*

The last sentence of this quotation describes Jesus being taken up to heaven. This is called the **ascension**. Many Christians remember the ascension on Ascension Sunday through worship, hymn-singing and prayers.

 The ascension of Jesus depicted in a stained glass window in a Nottinghamshire church

BUILD YOUR SKILLS

1. Copy and complete the following table for the four important terms from the life and death of Jesus given in this unit.

Term	What does it mean?	Why is it important for Christians?
Last Supper		
Crucifixion		
Resurrection		
Ascension		

2. Consider whether you agree or disagree with each of the following statements and explain why.
   a 'Only Christians should be allowed to celebrate Christmas.'
   b 'Easter is about the death of Jesus, not about Easter eggs.'
   c 'Jesus did not exist.'
   d 'Jesus has no importance in today's world.'

3. Read Luke 22–24, taking notes about the key events. What can Christians learn about Jesus from these events? Write two paragraphs and explain your reasons using quotations. **STRETCH**

SUMMARY

- Christians believe that Jesus is both God and man. They believe he was crucified, rose from the dead and, after a short time, ascended into heaven.
- Christians claim that all who believe in Jesus can have eternal life.
- Jesus taught people how to pray and how to have a relationship with God through love and worship.

EXAM-STYLE QUESTIONS

a Outline **three** events in the last days of Jesus' life. (3)

d 'Jesus' crucifixion was the most important event in history.' Evaluate this statement considering arguments for and against. In your response you should:
   - refer to Christian teachings
   - reach a justified conclusion. (15)

1.5 Salvation

What is salvation?

Jesus Christ came to bring what Christians call **salvation**, by saving them from their sin and reuniting them with God. The Bible says:

> ❝For God did not send his Son into the world to condemn the world, but **to save the world** through him.❞
> *(John 3: 17)*

So what does this mean? Christians believe that everyone was created for relationship with God. Whether the account of Adam and Eve is taken as literal or not, it does show that humanity had a perfect relationship with God until they chose to walk away from it. Some Christians suggest that because Adam and Eve sinned against God, all humanity is automatically sinful and in need of salvation. Other Christians believe that people are not automatically sinful, but that all will sin at one time or another.

In many ways the nature of sin is not the primary focus of Christianity. The primary focus is on the God who loved humanity so much that he sent Jesus to die on the cross so that whoever believed in him would have a relationship with God forever (*John 3: 16*).

SPECIFICATION FOCUS

The nature and significance of salvation and the role of Christ within salvation: law, sin, grace and Spirit, the role of Christ in salvation including John 3: 10–21 and Acts 4: 8–12; the nature and significance of atonement within Christianity and its link to salvation.

USEFUL TERMS

Atonement: the action of restoring a relationship; in Christianity, Jesus' death and resurrection restores the relationship between God and human beings

Grace: undeserved love

Law: guidelines as to how people should behave

Repentance: to say sorry for, and turn away from, any wrongdoing

Salvation: being saved from sin and the consequences of sin; going to heaven

A A modern stained glass window in St Edmundsbury Cathedral showing an angel banishing Adam and Eve from the Garden of Eden

Law, sin, grace, and Spirit

Christians believe that people were separated from the love of God because they did wrongful things (sin) and disobeyed the **law** of God. The law consists of guidelines on how people should behave and the most famous part is the Ten Commandments (*Exodus 20*).

However, Jesus taught that the law was not enough to save people (*Matthew 5: 20*) and he was critical of those who congratulated themselves on keeping the law (*Luke 5: 32*). What was needed was **repentance** and an acceptance that righteousness was not possible without the **grace** that came through Jesus.

In other words, people might think that by trying really hard to be good they can achieve God's favour, but this is not the case in the Christian faith. In the book of Acts, the Apostle Peter explains that the only way that people can be saved is through Jesus:

> ❛**Salvation is found in no one else**, for there is no other name under heaven given to mankind by which we must be saved. ❜
> (*Acts 4: 12*)

Christians therefore believe that they must turn away from sin, receive the freely given gift of grace through Jesus, and have faith in him, in order to be saved. Christians believe that, when they make this decision for the first time, they also welcome the Holy Spirit into their lives.

B *Christ of Saint John of the Cross by Salvador Dalí (1951)*

What is atonement?

Christians believe that, because Jesus died to save humanity from sin, the relationship between God and humanity was restored. This is called **atonement** or, more literally, 'at-one-ment'. God and humans are 'at one' because of Jesus.

Christians believe Jesus died as an act of love to save humanity, even though humanity did not deserve it. His love is called grace, which means undeserved love.

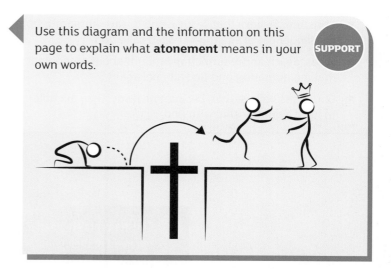

Use this diagram and the information on this page to explain what **atonement** means in your own words.

SUPPORT

What is the significance of atonement and salvation within Christianity?

- Christians believe Jesus' death allows humans to have eternal life.

- Christians have a moral duty to live their lives as Jesus lived his, loving and caring for each other: 'I have set you an example that you should do as I have done for you.' (*John 13: 15*). In this way, humans are saved from the power and consequences of sin.

- God and humanity can have their loving relationship restored. Christians regularly repent of any wrong-doing and believe that, because of Jesus, they are forgiven by God.

BUILD YOUR SKILLS

1   Complete the following table concerning salvation:

Term	What does it mean?	Why is it important for Christians?
Sin		
Salvation		
Sacrifice		
Atonement		

2   Read through this topic carefully and write an answer to each of the following questions, making sure you explain your points:

 STRETCH

   a Why did the Son of God come to earth as a human?
   b Why doesn't God just forgive sins?
   c Do you believe humans need the salvation that Jesus offers?
   d How does atonement link to salvation?

? EXAM-STYLE QUESTIONS

a Outline **three** features of salvation for Christians. (3)

c Explain **two** reasons why salvation is important for Christians today. In your answer you must refer to a source of wisdom and authority. (5)

SUMMARY

- Christians believe that Jesus came to save humanity from the consequences of sin; this is called salvation.

- Jesus' death and resurrection brought about atonement – making humanity and God 'at one' again.

- Christians believe that, because of Jesus, they are able to have a relationship with God.

C Christians pray regularly to repent of their wrong-doings and to receive forgiveness from God

1.6 Christian Eschatology

SPECIFICATION FOCUS

Christian Eschatology: divergent Christian teachings about life after death including the nature and significance of resurrection, judgement, heaven, and hell and purgatory with reference to the 39 Articles of Religion and Catholic teachings; how beliefs about life after death are shown in the Bible including reference to 2 Corinthians 5: 1–10 and divergent understandings as to why they are important for Christians today.

Eschatology is an area of Christian teaching which is all about life after death. All living things eventually die, but Christians believe that there is another life beyond this physical life. Here are a few Christian beliefs.

> When we die, the souls of the good go to a wonderful paradise called **heaven** to be with God.

> When we die, the souls of the wicked go to a place of eternal punishment called **hell**.

> On the Last Day, God will raise the dead in bodily form. This is resurrection.

The Bible teaches that all who believe in Jesus will have eternal life:

> ❝For God so loved the world that he gave his one and only Son, that **whoever believes in him shall not perish but have eternal life**.❞
> *(John 3: 16)*

Christians think of life after death in divergent ways:

- The most common view is that everyone has an **immortal soul** that leaves our physical body when we die and goes to God in heaven, or otherwise goes to hell. This view holds that followers of Jesus who die will go to heaven and those who are not followers of Jesus will go to hell. Christians differ on what they think heaven and hell will be like.

- Some Christians believe that Jesus died to forgive all sins, and so everyone (not just Christians) will live forever in heaven. This is called **universalism**.

- Many Catholics believe in **purgatory**, where the dead are purified of their sins before going to heaven.

Christians also vary on whether the above happens as soon as people die, or at the end of time, on what Christians call the **Day of Judgement**.

Heaven

Heaven is the place where Christians believe that they will spend the afterlife. It is not described in detail in the Bible, so Christians have different views about what it will be like. Some believe that it is a physical place, whilst others believe it is a state of being spiritually united with God. The Bible teaches that heaven is a place of everlasting peace and joy for those who believe in Jesus:

> ❝Then I saw "a new heaven and a new earth" [...] I saw the Holy City, the new Jerusalem, coming down out of heaven from God [...] He will wipe every tear from their eyes. There will be no more death or mourning or crying or pain...❞
> *(Revelation 21: 1–4)*

USEFUL TERMS

Eschatology: an area of Christian theology which is concerned with life after death

Heaven: place of eternal paradise where Christians believe they will spend the afterlife

Hell: place of punishment and separation from God

Immortal soul: a soul that lives on after the death of the body

Day of Judgement: God assesses a person's life and actions

Purgatory: a place where the souls of the dead are cleansed and prepared for heaven

Universalism: the belief that because of the love and mercy of God everyone will go to heaven

A

Hell

Many Christians believe in hell, a place of punishment and separation from God. Some Christians do not believe in hell, and instead believe that those who are not followers of Jesus would simply cease to exist when they die. Like heaven, the descriptions of hell in the Bible are not detailed:

> ‘He will punish those who do not know God and do not obey the gospel of our Lord Jesus. They will be punished with everlasting destruction...’
> *(2 Thessalonians 1: 8–9)*

Purgatory

Purgatory, from the Latin word *purgare* meaning ‘make clean’, is a concept mainly associated with the Catholic Church. It is a place (or state of mind) where the souls of those who have died go to be purified until they are made clean from their sins and can then go to heaven. The *Catechism of the Catholic Church* describes it in this way:

> ‘All who die in God’s grace and friendship, but still imperfectly purified, are indeed assured of their eternal salvation; but **after death they undergo purification**, so as to achieve the holiness necessary to enter the joy of heaven.’
> *Catechism of the Catholic Church, 1030*

However, this is not a view held by Protestant Christians. The *39 Articles of Religion*, which is an ancient statement of the beliefs and teachings of the Church of England, says the following about purgatory:

> ‘The Romish Doctrine concerning Purgatory [...] is a fond thing vainly invented, and grounded upon no warranty of Scripture, but rather repugnant to the Word of God’
> *(Article 22, 39 Articles of Religion)*

This is a strongly worded criticism of the idea of purgatory:
- ‘**Fond thing vainly invented**’ means they believe it has been made up
- ‘**Grounded upon no warranty of Scripture**’ means they don’t believe it is backed up by the Bible
- ‘**Repugnant**’ means unacceptable.

Judgement

Christians believe that God is just, fair and merciful. They believe in the Day of Judgement, when God will judge all people according to how they lived their lives on earth and to give them the afterlife they deserve.

> ‘And I saw the dead, great and small, standing before the throne [...] the dead were judged according to what they had done...’
> *(Revelation 20: 12)*

Christians also believe in the Second Coming, when Jesus will return to earth. This will be the time for judgement and the establishment of God’s kingdom.

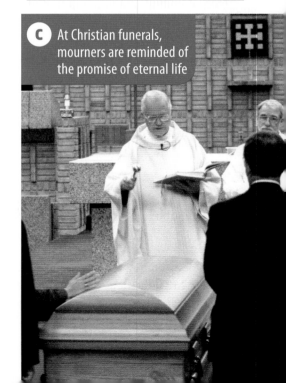

C At Christian funerals, mourners are reminded of the promise of eternal life

Resurrection

For Christians, the resurrection of Jesus has made sure that there will be an afterlife for all who believe in him. In *1 Corinthians 15: 12*, St Paul wrote, 'But if it is preached that Christ has been raised from the dead, how can some of you say that there is no resurrection of the dead?' Paul argues that if Christians believe that Jesus rose from the dead, then they must believe they can look forward to an afterlife.

Therefore, many Christians believe that, at the end of time, God will raise their bodies to life again, as he did with Jesus' body. The appearances of Jesus after his resurrection are usually thought by Christians to be the strongest evidence that this will happen. According to the Bible, when Jesus appeared to his disciples after death they were able to touch him *(Luke 24: 39)*. Paul uses the metaphor of buildings to explain what will happen to the body after death:

> **‘**For we know that if the earthly tent we live in is destroyed, we have a building from God, an eternal house in heaven, not built by human hands.**’**
> *(2 Corinthians 5: 1)*

In other words, the physical human body eventually dies, but a resurrected body goes on forever.

What do you think Paul means by saying that because Jesus rose from the dead they can have an afterlife? **STRETCH**

Why is life after death important for Christians today?

- Jesus said that those who believe in him would have life after death.
- Life after death is a reward for faithful people.
- Life after death offers hope for the future.
- Life after death allows Christians to be with God forever.

 COMPARE AND CONTRAST

In your exam, you could be asked to **compare and contrast** Christian beliefs on life after death with the beliefs of another religion you are studying. You should consider the similarities and differences between them.

 BUILD YOUR SKILLS

1 Look at images **A** and **B**. How successful are they at depicting heaven and hell? Explain your reasons and refer to Christian beliefs.

2 Here are some divergent views about life after death.
- 'If God really loves us, everyone should go to heaven.'
- 'There is no life after death. When we die, we just die.'
- 'People who are bad should go to hell as a punishment.'
  a Consider whether you agree or disagree with each statement and explain why.
  b How might a religious believer respond to each statement?

 SUMMARY

- Christian belief in the afterlife is very important and is connected to beliefs about Jesus' own death and resurrection and what that means for Christians.
- There are divergent views within Christianity about the nature of heaven and hell, purgatory, and the resurrection of the body.

EXAM-STYLE QUESTIONS

c Explain **two** reasons why some Christians believe in the resurrection of the body. In your answer you must refer to a source of wisdom and authority. (5)

d 'There is no life after death.' Evaluate this statement considering arguments for and against. In your response you should:
- refer to Christian teachings
- refer to different Christian points of view
- reach a justified conclusion. (15)

What is God like?

There are two characteristics of God's nature that are particularly important in helping Christians to approach the problem of evil and suffering:

- **Omnipotence** – God is all-powerful
- **Benevolence** – God is all-good/loving.

Christians believe that, if God is all-powerful, then nothing is impossible for him; if he is all-good, then he is loving and cannot do wrong. In the Bible, God's love and power means that he not only *wants* to help people, but he is also *able* to:

> ❝The Lord works righteousness and justice for all the oppressed❞
> *(Psalm 103: 6)*

What is the problem of evil and suffering?

Evil is the opposite of good: it causes pain, grief and damage. Evil and suffering can be on a large scale or a smaller, personal scale, as almost everyone experiences pain and suffering at different times in their lives.

There are two types of evil and suffering:

- **Natural evil**: suffering caused by nature that is beyond human control.
- **Moral evil**: deliberately evil actions by human beings that cause suffering to others.

SPECIFICATION FOCUS

The problem of evil/suffering and a loving and righteous God: the problems it raises for Christians about the nature of God including reference to omnipotence and benevolence including Psalm 103; how the problem may cause believers to question their faith or the existence of God; the nature and examples of natural suffering, moral suffering.

USEFUL TERMS

Benevolence: all-good

Moral evil: suffering caused by humans, such as war

Natural evil: suffering caused by natural events, such as earthquakes

Omnipotence: all-powerful

Earthquakes

Disease

Famine

Volcanoes

A Examples of natural evil; image shows a man rescuing an unknown girl from flood waters in Bangkok

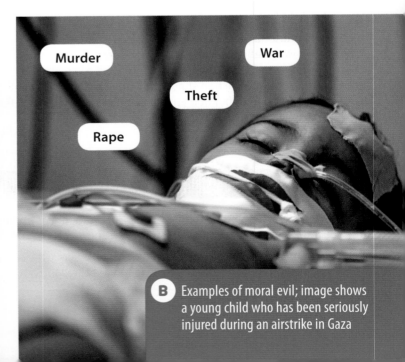

Murder

War

Theft

Rape

B Examples of moral evil; image shows a young child who has been seriously injured during an airstrike in Gaza

How might the problem lead some people to question God's existence?

The existence of evil and suffering in the world is one of the strongest arguments against the existence of God. If it is true that God is all-powerful and all-loving, it seems logical that he should prevent evil and suffering. Since evil and suffering *do* exist, some people have concluded that God does *not*.

The problem can be expressed in this way:

- God is thought to be all-loving (benevolent) and all-powerful (omnipotent).
- If God is benevolent he would *want* to remove evil and suffering.
- If God is omnipotent he would *be able* to remove evil and suffering.
- Therefore, both God and evil cannot exist together, yet evil *does* exist.
- Therefore, God cannot exist.

This can be illustrated in the form of an inconsistent triad (see image **C**).

The existence of evil

Inconsistent Triad

God is all-powerful

God is all-good

C The inconsistent triad; if you combine any two points of the triangle, the third point is disproved

Why does the problem cause believers to question their faith?

The problem of evil challenges the existence and characteristics of God. This can cause believers to doubt their beliefs, especially if they or their loved ones are experiencing pain. In times of doubt, a Christian might ask:

- If God exists but isn't all-powerful and all-loving, how can I worship him?
- If God is not all-powerful or not all-loving, is that a God I want to believe in?
- If God is all-powerful and all-loving, how could he allow suffering?

Many people find it difficult to understand what it means to say that God is all-loving. Some believe God should only love those who are good. If God is all-loving, does he love tyrants and mass murderers? **SUPPORT**

BUILD YOUR SKILLS

1 What are the two kinds of evil? Can you give five examples of each kind? **SUPPORT**

2 Write down a potential problem of God's omnipotence.
  a How would a non-religious person respond?
  b How would a Christian respond?

3 a Is a God who is not all-powerful still worthy of a Christian's worship? Why/why not? **STRETCH**
  b If God is benevolent, can he ever be bad?

SUMMARY

- Christians believe that God is omnipotent and benevolent.
- There are two types of evil in the world: natural evil and moral evil.
- Some people question whether the existence of evil and suffering shows that God either does not exist or is not all-powerful or all-loving.

EXAM-STYLE QUESTIONS

a Outline **three** features of the problem of evil and suffering. (3)
b Explain **two** types of evil and suffering. (4)

Divergent solutions to the problem of evil

Biblical solutions

In the Bible there are many references to evil and suffering, and suggestions that suffering is part of life. This is sometimes linked to the existence of a personal force of evil, given different names in the history of Christianity: the Devil, **Satan** or Lucifer. In Christianity, Satan (which means 'the adversary') was one of God's angels who had rebelled against the rule of God. In the Book of Job, a good man and a believer in God suffers great hardship and tragedy after God is challenged by Satan.

> 'What I feared has come upon me;
> **what I dreaded has happened to me.**
> I have no peace, no quietness.
> I have no rest, but only turmoil. '
> *(Job 3: 25–26)*

In the midst of Job's suffering, God tells him that the problem of evil and suffering has no simple answer and that he must trust God. In the end, all turns out well for Job.

> 'The fear of the Lord – that is wisdom,
> and to shun evil is understanding. '
> *(Job 28: 28)*

> 'I know that you [God] can do all things;
> no purpose of yours can be thwarted. '
> *(Job 42: 2)*

SPECIFICATION FOCUS

Divergent solutions offered to the problem of evil/suffering and a loving and righteous God: biblical, theoretical and practical including reference to Psalm 119, Job, free will, vale of soul-making, prayer, and charity; the success of solutions to the problem.

USEFUL TERMS

Satan: 'the adversary'; one of God's angels who rebelled against the rule of God

STRETCH

The story of Job is very complex and raises questions. If God is all-powerful, why does he allow Satan to tell him what to do or exist at all? If God is all-loving, why does he permit the suffering of a good man? The answer seems to be that God is mysterious and humans are not allowed to know everything. What do you think?

A This child has no parents and no home, and has to beg on the streets of Mumbai in order to survive. For some people, the question of why suffering happens has no easy answer.

The Book of Psalms is a collection of songs and prayers dedicated to God in which the theme of suffering is very common. Some of the psalms express feelings of abandonment by God:

> ❝Save me, O God, for the waters have come up to my neck. [...] I am worn out calling for help; my throat is parched. **My eyes fail, looking for my God.**❞
> *(Psalm 69: 1, 3)*

Psalm 119 acknowledges the existence of suffering as part of life, but also states that God is trustworthy:

> ❝My comfort in my suffering is this: Your promise preserves my life.❞
> *(Psalm 119: 50)*

> ❝My soul faints with longing for your salvation, but I have put my hope in your word.❞
> *(Psalm 119: 81)*

Other psalms praise God for his help in times of trouble:

> ❝**I called to the Lord**, who is worthy of praise,
> **and I have been saved** from my enemies.❞
> *(Psalm 18: 3)*

The Bible teaches that, one day, God will end all evil and suffering for good:

> ❝**He will wipe every tear from their eyes**. There will be no more death or mourning or crying or pain, for the old order of things has passed away.❞
> *(Revelation 21: 4)*

Biblical solutions to evil and suffering encourage Christians to believe:
- Suffering is part of life.
- Christians can pray to God to get comfort in their suffering and they should praise God for his help in times of trouble.
- God is love, but sometimes it's hard to understand why God doesn't intervene. Faith sometimes involves trust without understanding.
- One day all suffering will come to an end.

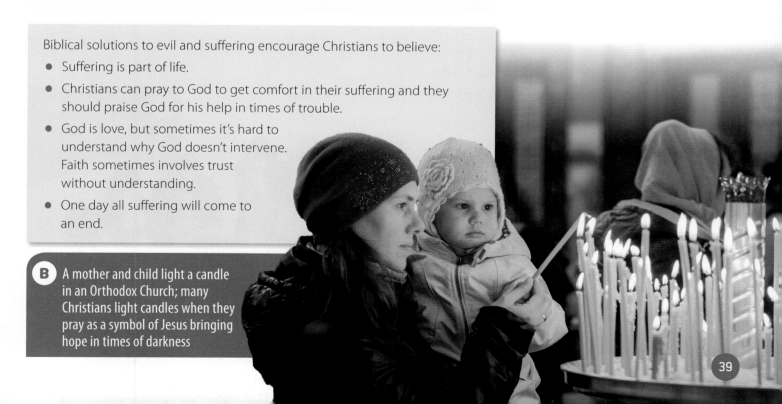

B A mother and child light a candle in an Orthodox Church; many Christians light candles when they pray as a symbol of Jesus bringing hope in times of darkness

Theoretical solutions

Christians may respond by looking at what is behind the problem and how it may be resolved. In the Bible, *Genesis 2–3* highlights this very clearly by showing that evil and suffering can be the result of human free will. The first human beings, Adam and Eve, used their free will to disobey God. When they did so, evil and suffering were brought into the world and they were separated from God.

> ❛So the Lord God banished him [Adam] from the garden of Eden to work the ground from which he had been taken.❜
> *(Genesis 3: 23)*

Some Christians go further and say that this world is a **vale of soul-making** – an environment where everything that is necessary for human growth and development can be found. For instance, in the midst of evil and suffering there are opportunities to do good, or to do bad, to choose the right way or the wrong way.

Some Christians say that the world provides all they need to choose to be good or bad people. Can you think of some examples?

SUPPORT

Theoretical solutions to evil and suffering encourage Christians to believe:

- God gives humans free will to act as they wish.
- Humans may choose to do evil or inflict suffering and that's why evil exists.
- Suffering helps people to develop good characteristics.

Practical responses

Christians believe that suffering is part of life, and they have a duty to respond to this practically:

- They can develop positive qualities such as compassion and kindness, courage and honesty.
- They can help each other to make the world a better place and learn how to improve things for themselves and future generations.
- They can help through involvement in charity work.
- They can pray for God's help and encouragement.

Many Christians pray for those who are suffering. This is called **intercession**. They believe that they can change the impacts of evil and suffering by praying to God on behalf of those who are suffering.

Practical responses to evil and suffering encourage Christians to believe:

- Christians can develop positive qualities such as compassion.
- Suffering is part of life but help can be given.
- Christians can help by praying and doing charitable work.

C Many Christians meet together to pray in times of difficulty

The success of solutions to the problem

	Strengths	Weaknesses
Biblical solutions	<ul><li>Help Christians to understand God more clearly and trust that he will make everything right in the end.</li><li>Help Christians to believe that God acts for good in the world.</li></ul>	<ul><li>People in the Bible still experience suffering, and God does not always stop it.</li><li>It can be harder to trust God when things aren't going well.</li></ul>
Theoretical solutions	<ul><li>Explain that evil and suffering come from human free will, not from God.</li><li>Encourage Christians to use times of evil and suffering to make the right choices and grow closer to God.</li></ul>	<ul><li>God created the universe, therefore he must be responsible for the existence of evil.</li><li>It may not be reasonable to expect people to respond well in times of suffering.</li></ul>
Practical responses	Christians would say that practical responses to evil and suffering are not a 'solution' to the problem, but they can be successful in easing suffering. Christians believe suffering is a reality of life, and they have a choice to respond practically to help with the consequences.	

BUILD YOUR SKILLS

1 Of the solutions to the problem of evil and suffering,
  a which is the most successful?
  b which is the least successful?
     Give your reasons.

2 Would the world be a better place if there was no evil and suffering? Discuss with a partner.

3 Look through a newspaper and make a list of all the news stories involving suffering. Then answer these questions:
  STRETCH
  - What was the suffering shown in each incident?
  - Was the suffering in each case an act of nature or caused by human actions?
  - How could the suffering in each case have been prevented?
  - Do you think that prayer would be useful in these situations? Think carefully about what you think prayer accomplishes.

SUMMARY

- The problem of evil and suffering challenges the existence of God because if God is all-good and all-powerful, why doesn't he put an end to suffering?

- Christians respond to evil and suffering in different ways, including reading the Bible, praying, and working to relieve suffering.

- Christians might argue that God gave humans free will, and that evil and suffering are the consequences of human action.

EXAM-STYLE QUESTIONS

c Explain **two** different Christian solutions to the problem of evil and suffering. In your answer you must refer to a source of wisdom and authority. (5)

d 'God is not responsible for suffering in the world.' Evaluate this statement considering arguments for and against. In your response you should:
  - refer to Christian teachings
  - refer to different Christian points of view
  - reach a justified conclusion. (15)

Revision

BUILD YOUR SKILLS

Look at the list of 'I can' statements below and think carefully about how confident you are. Use the following code to rate each of the statements. Be honest!

Green – very confident. What is your evidence for this?

Orange – quite confident. What is your target? Be specific.

Red – not confident. What is your target? Be specific.

A self-assessment revision checklist is available on *Kerboodle*

I can...

- Explain what the Trinity is and why the oneness of God is significant

- Give reasons why the Trinity is significant in Christianity

- Give quotations from the Bible and the Nicene Creed about the Trinity

- Explain the characteristics of the Trinity – Father, Son, and Holy Spirit

- Describe how the Trinity is reflected in Christian worship and belief today

- Describe the biblical account of creation

- Explain two different ways that Christians interpret creation

- Explain the role of the Word and Spirit in creation with reference to sources of wisdom and authority

- Explain the importance of creation for Christians today

- Explain the meaning of the incarnation with reference to a source of wisdom and authority

- Explain why the incarnation is so important to Christians

- Describe the key events in the last days of Jesus' life (including the Last Supper, betrayal, arrest, trial, crucifixion, resurrection and ascension of Jesus), with reference to the accounts of these within the Bible

- Give reasons why these events are significant, and describe what they show about the person of Jesus

- Explain the idea of salvation and why it is so important within Christianity

- Explain the role of Jesus in salvation including reference to a source of wisdom and authority

- Define atonement, and explain how it links to salvation

- Explain different Christian views on life after death

- Explain the meaning and significance of resurrection, judgement, heaven, hell and purgatory with reference to sources of wisdom and authority

- Describe the problem of evil and suffering, with reference to natural and moral evil

- Explain the problems suffering raises for Christians about the nature of God

- Explain how evil and suffering can challenge religious belief

- Describe different solutions to the problem of evil and suffering, including biblical, theoretical and practical solutions

- Discuss the success of the solutions to the problem of evil.

Exam practice

On these exam practice pages you will see example answers for each of the exam question types: **a**, **b**, **c**, and **d**. You can find out more about these on pages 6–10.

• Question 'a'

*Question **a** is AO1 – this tests your knowledge and understanding.*

> (a) Outline **three** features of the biblical story of creation. (3)

Student response

God created the earth in six days and then he rested.

Improved student response

The biblical story of creation says that God is the creator. He created the earth in six days and then rested. He looked at his creation and decided that it was good.

 Over to you! Give yourself three minutes on the clock and have a go at answering this question. Remember, this question type requires you to provide three facts or short ideas: you don't need to explain them or express any opinions.

✓ **WHAT WENT WELL**

This student has correctly identified an aspect of the biblical story of creation.

! **HOW TO IMPROVE**

This answer does not outline three features of the biblical story of creation. For a high level response, three distinct features should be given. See the 'improved student response' opposite for suggested corrections.

• Question 'b'

*Question **b** is AO1 – this tests your knowledge and understanding.*

> (a) Explain **two** Christian beliefs about the incarnation. (4)

Student response

The Son of God came to earth, and he was born a human called Jesus.

Improved student response

The incarnation is a core Christian doctrine which holds that the Son of God came to earth, and he was born a human called Jesus.

Christians also believe that the incarnation took place for a special purpose, which was to restore the relationship between God and humanity which had been destroyed by sin.

 Over to you! Give yourself four minutes on the clock and have a go at answering this question. Remember, in order to 'explain' something, you need to **develop** your points. See page 9 for a reminder of how to do this.

✓ **WHAT WENT WELL**

The student has given a correct Christian belief and explained it.

! **HOW TO IMPROVE**

The question asks for two Christian beliefs about the incarnation, and the answer only contains one. For a high level response, students should explain two Christian beliefs about the incarnation. See the 'improved student response' opposite for suggested corrections.

• Question 'c'

*Question **c** is AO1 – this tests your knowledge and understanding.*

> (c)   Explain **two** different Christian beliefs about life after death. In your answer you must refer to a source of wisdom and authority. (5)

Student response

Roman Catholic Christians believe in the existence of purgatory, a place where the souls of the dead go to be purified after death. This is so that they can achieve holiness before entering heaven.

The Church of England does not believe in the existence of purgatory however, and argues that it is not referred to in the Bible.

Improved student response

Roman Catholic Christians believe in the existence of purgatory, a place where the souls of the dead go to be purified after death. This is so that they can achieve holiness before entering heaven.

The Church of England does not believe in the existence of purgatory however, and argues that it is not referred to in the Bible. The 39 Articles of Religion claim that it has been 'invented' (Article 22).

 Over to you! Give yourself five minutes on the clock and have a go at answering this question. Remember, you need to write two developed points, one of which needs to be supported by a source of wisdom and authority.

 ✓ WHAT WENT WELL

This student has correctly explained two different Christian beliefs about life after death.

 ! HOW TO IMPROVE

The student hasn't referred to a source of wisdom and authority. See the 'improved student response' opposite for a suggested correction.

• Question 'd'

*Question **d** is AO2 – this tests your ability to evaluate. Some d questions also carry an extra three marks for spelling, punctuation and grammar.*

> **In this question, 3 of the marks awarded will be for your spelling, punctuation and grammar and your use of specialist terminology.**
>
> *(d) 'Christianity provides no solutions to the problem of evil and suffering.' Evaluate this statement considering arguments for and against. In your response you should:
> - refer to Christian teachings
> - refer to different Christian points of view
> - reach a justified conclusion. (15)

Student response

If God was omnibenevolent he would not let us suffer. Christains will teach that God knows why people suffer, consequently he uses suffering to show his love and faithfulness to people and this should give them faith.

The Catholic Church teaches that it is a Christian responsibility to respond in practical ways to ease the suffering of others. Because of this many Christians will choose jobs which show they care and help other people.

However some Christians could argue that evil and suffering has nothing to do with God as in the Bible it says evil is a result of the actions of Adam and Eve. Therefore it is not a Christian's duty to provide solutions for the problem of evil and suffering.

Improved student response

For many Christians, the way they respond to suffering is a very important part of their faith. They believe that suffering brings them closer to God as <u>Christians</u> will teach that God knows why people suffer, consequently he uses suffering to show his love and faithfulness to his followers. It could be argued, however, that the existence of evil and suffering in the world challenges the claim that Christianity has anything to offer, because the problem is yet to be solved.

In contrast to this view, the existence of evil and suffering is seen by many as proof that Christians have a duty to help each other and relieve suffering in whichever way is needed. The Catholic Church teaches that it is a Christian responsibility to respond in practical ways to ease the suffering of others through charitable actions. Because of this many Christians will choose jobs which show they care and want to help other people.

However, some Christians think that the problem of evil and suffering is a direct result of the misuse of human free will and therefore has nothing to do with God. The story of the Fall places responsibility for suffering on humanity: "Cursed is the ground because of you" (Genesis 3: 17), which suggests that it is the responsibility of humans to find solutions to reducing suffering in the world.

On balance, it seems to me that the Christian faith does have solutions to offer. Salvation can only be achieved if Christians consider their actions and how they support others and this is most evident when faced with suffering.

 Over to you! Give yourself 15 minutes on the clock and have a go at answering this question. Remember to refer back to the original statement in your writing when you give different points of view, and make sure you cover each of the bullet points given in the question. Allow three minutes to check your spelling, punctuation and grammar and use of specialist terminology.

BUILD YOUR SKILLS

In your exams, you'll need to make sure you use religious terminology correctly. Do you know the meaning of the following important terms for this topic?

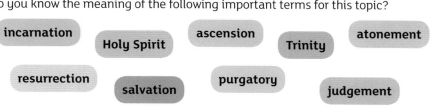

incarnation　Holy Spirit　ascension　Trinity　atonement　resurrection　salvation　purgatory　judgement

 WHAT WENT WELL

This is a low level response. The student understands that they must explain different Christian viewpoints.

 HOW TO IMPROVE

Both sides of this argument lack detailed understanding, and there aren't any clear links back to the question. It could be improved with a more logical chain of reasoning, and more detail, including specific references to sources of wisdom and authority. There is also a spelling error. See the 'improved student response' opposite for suggested corrections.

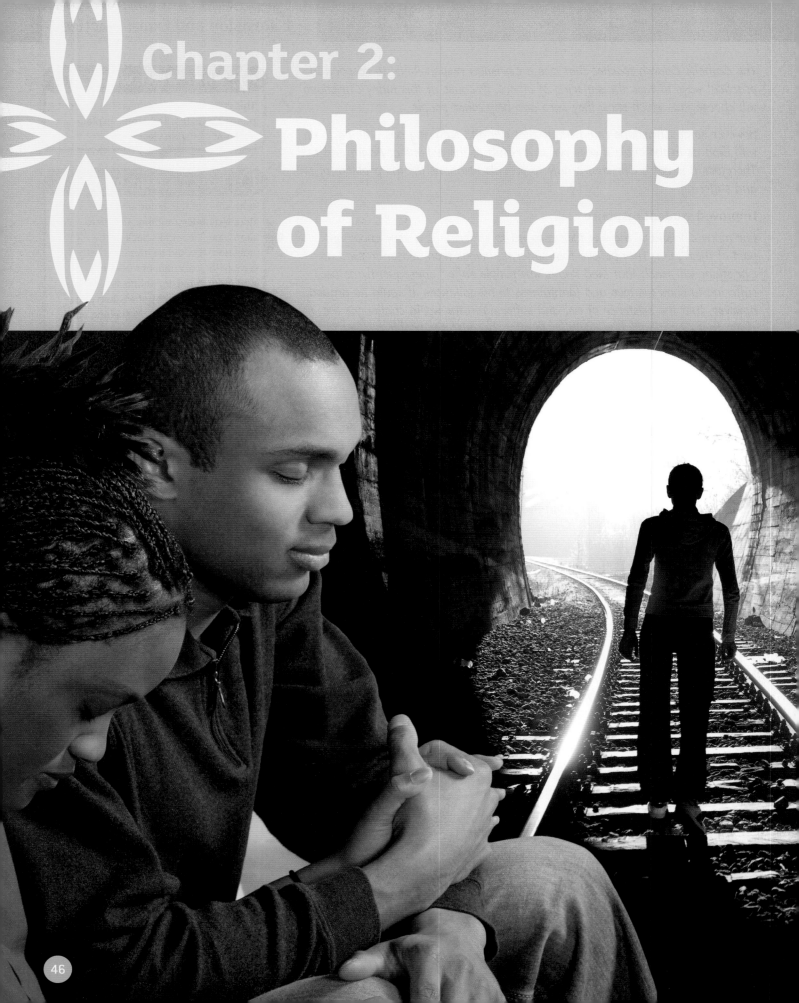

Chapter 2:
Philosophy of Religion

2.1 Revelation

What is revelation?

A **revelation** is when a truth is revealed that was previously hidden. For Christians, the word refers to the way God makes himself known to human beings.

There are different types of revelation – for example, a person might experience God in a particular event, such as a vision or a miracle (see units 2.2–2.4). One of the ways that Christians believe God reveals himself is through the Bible. They believe it is a record of how God has revealed himself to humanity.

Revelation as proof of God's existence

It is important to realise that Christians do not believe God reveals himself in order to prove his existence. They believe he reveals himself to help humanity to understand him more clearly, worship him for who he is, and follow his example. In doing so however, many Christians would argue that revelations like this can prove that God exists.

How is revelation shown in the Bible?

There are many revelations in the Bible that show something about the nature of God. One very important way is when God makes a **covenant** (a special agreement) with his people. Christians believe that, through covenants, God has expressed his love for humans and his desire to have a relationship with them.

Covenant with Noah

According to the book of Genesis, there was a time of great evil in the human race, and so God sent a great flood to sweep away every living thing. However, a man named Noah was 'blameless' (*Genesis 6: 9*), so God saved him, his family, and every species of creature. After the flood, God blessed Noah and promised that he would never flood the earth again.

SPECIFICATION FOCUS

Revelation as proof of the existence of God: Revelation as shown in the Bible including in the covenants with Noah and Abraham and through Jesus including Hebrews 1: 1–4; divergent understandings of what revelation shows about the nature of God for Christians.

USEFUL TERMS

Covenant: an agreement between two parties, for example God and humanity

Revelation: when a truth is revealed that was previously hidden

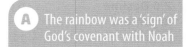

A The rainbow was a 'sign' of God's covenant with Noah

'As for you, be fruitful and increase in number [...] I now establish my covenant with you and with your descendants after you [...] never again will there be a flood to destroy the earth. '
(Genesis 9: 7–11)

What do these covenants tell us about what God is like? **SUPPORT**

Covenant with Abraham

Later in Genesis, Christians read about a man called Abraham – a descendant of Noah. The Bible teaches that God chose Abraham to have many descendants, and that these people would be God's holy people who would bless all the nations of the earth. He made Abraham this promise:

'As for me, this is my covenant with you: You will be the father of many nations [...] I will establish my covenant as an everlasting covenant between me and you and your descendants [...] to be your God [...]. The whole land of Canaan [...] I will give as an everlasting possession to you and your descendants [...]. As for you, you must keep my covenant [...] You are to undergo circumcision, and it will be the sign of the covenant between me and you. '
(Genesis 17: 4, 7–11)

Covenants between God and humanity in the Bible **STRETCH** usually have three aspects to them:
- God agrees to do something
- Humans agree to do something
- A 'sign' reminds them of their agreement.

Can you identify these three aspects in the covenants described here?

Covenant through Jesus

Christians believe that God made a final covenant with humanity by promising eternal life to all who believe in Jesus. Paul describes this in the book of Hebrews:

'In the past God spoke to our ancestors through the prophets at many times and in various ways, but **in these last days he has spoken to us by his Son**, whom he appointed heir of all things, and through whom also he made the universe. '
(Hebrews 1: 1–2)

Moses and Abraham are examples of **prophets** **SUPPORT** in the Old Testament. A prophet is a person who is chosen by God to speak on behalf of God.

According to Paul, the God who made a covenant with Moses and Abraham is the same God who came to earth as Jesus. Because he was both fully God and fully human, Jesus made it possible for humans to really see and hear God. Because of this, Christians believe Jesus himself is the most important revelation of all.

B *Christ the Redeemer, a statue of Jesus in Rio de Janeiro, Brazil*

What does revelation show about the nature of God for Christians?

Christians believe that the revelation of God as described in the Bible shows the following about the nature of God:

God loves humanity
He wants to have a relationship with humans and he ultimately came to earth in order to reveal himself to the world.

C The nature of God. Detail from *Creation of the Sun, Moon and Planets*, painted on the ceiling of the Sistine Chapel by Michelangelo (c.1511CE–1512CE)

'For God so loved the world that he gave his one and only Son, that whoever believes in him shall not perish but have eternal life.'
(John 3: 16)

God is holy
He helps humans to be free from sin so that they can know him.

God is eternal
God is outside of time. He has revealed himself to humans, and through Jesus he has enabled humans to have eternal life with him.

BUILD YOUR SKILLS

1   In your own words, explain what revelation means for Christians. Use the following words: Bible, covenant, Jesus.

2   a   Write a sentence or two linking the covenant through Jesus with the idea of salvation (see 1.5).
    b   What are the features of the new 'agreement' between God and humanity?

3   What would a non-religious person argue about revelation as described in this unit? Write a paragraph explaining.   **STRETCH**

SUMMARY

- Christians believe that God makes himself known to humanity through revelation, as shown in the Bible.

- Revelation shows that God loves humans and wants a relationship with them.

? EXAM-STYLE QUESTIONS

a   Outline **three** Christian beliefs about the revelation of God. (3)

b   Explain **two** reasons why revelation might prove the existence of God to Christians. (4)

2.2 Visions

What are visions?

For Christians, a religious **vision** is a way God sometimes reveals himself. It can involve seeing or hearing God, other holy people, or angels, or it might take another form that is personal to the believer's context. It may be something a Christian sees physically, or in the imagination, such as a dream.

Why are visions important?

Visions are important because they can:

- tell people of God's plans
- show people that God loves them
- encourage a person to take action or change their life
- strengthen faith in God.

Biblical examples of visions

There are many examples of visions in the Bible, particularly when God wants to make sure that his plans will happen. For example, God appears in a vision to Abraham (originally Abram), promising him land and many descendants. The Jewish people believe this promise was the beginning of God's special relationship with them. St Paul taught that Abraham's belief in God made him the model for all believers to follow.

> ❛After this, the word of the Lord came to Abram in a vision:
> "Do not be afraid, Abram.
> I am your shield,
> your very great reward."❜
> *(Genesis 15: 1)*

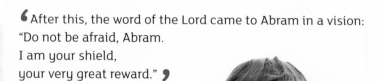

SPECIFICATION FOCUS

Visions as proof of the existence of God: the nature and importance of visions for Christians; biblical and non-biblical examples of visions including Genesis 15 and Matthew 17: 1–13; reasons why they might lead to belief in the existence of God and Christian responses to non-religious arguments (including atheist and Humanist) which maintain that visions are hallucinations and provide no proof that God exists; divergent understandings of what visions show about the nature of God for Christians.

USEFUL TERMS

Vision: seeing or hearing someone or something holy

How do you think Abraham would have felt about this vision? What would he have felt about God? **SUPPORT**

Look up the following accounts of visions in the Bible. Which do you think is most and least convincing? Explain your views. **STRETCH**

- Genesis 15: 1–5 – Abram's vision
- Genesis 28: 12–15 – Jacob's Ladder
- Matthew 17: 1–13 – the Transfiguration
- Saul's (Paul's) vision – Acts 9: 1–21

Non-biblical examples of visions

There have been many non-biblical examples of visions recorded throughout history.

Bernadette Soubirous

Some of the most famous visions occurred at Lourdes in France. In 1858, a 14-year-old girl called Bernadette Soubirous saw visions of the Virgin Mary, who told her to build a chapel for healing the sick. Now, millions of **pilgrims** visit the chapel every year and many have claimed that they have been miraculously healed.

Our Lady of Fátima

In 1916, three children – Lucia Santos, Jacinta Marto, and Francisco Marto – from Fátima in Portugal claimed to have seen an angel who taught them how to pray and worship. Then, in May 1917, they had a vision of the Virgin Mary. She promised to show them a miracle (for more on miracles, see 2.3).

As word spread, thousands of people flocked to Fátima to see the miracle. On 13 October 1917, they all saw the sun appearing in the form of a rotating disc, zigzagging across the sky. The Pope gave permission for Catholics to accept the visions as genuine and a chapel was built. Today, thousands of pilgrims visit Fátima.

A Bernadette Soubirous (1844–1879)

The Catholic Church declared Bernadette a saint in 1933. Do you think she really saw the Virgin Mary? Is there another explanation?

SUPPORT

Do visions lead to belief?

The non-religious viewpoint

- **Humanists** would argue that there is no physical or scientific proof that visions have taken place, and eyewitness accounts can be unreliable.
- Someone who already believes in God may want to have a religious experience or might more easily believe that a vision comes from God.
- There might be other explanations for the events, such as imagination, misunderstanding, or **hallucinations** caused by ill-health, drugs, or alcohol.
- An **atheist** could argue that even if a vision is believed to be genuine it does not mean that God exists.

The Christian viewpoint

- A vision can be a very powerful, personal experience that strengthens a person's faith.
- There are many recorded examples of religious visions in the Bible and throughout history which could lead people to consider God's existence.
- Many so-called visions are unexplainable without reference to God.
- Visions can change lives in dramatic ways, often to the benefit of others. Christians could attribute this positive change as the work of God.

B Every year, thousands of people visit and kneel at the shrine at Fátima

Divergent understandings about visions

Not all Christians believe that God sends visions to people today. Those who do would refer to verses in the Bible like the following:

> ❛In the last days, God says, I will pour out my Spirit on all people. Your sons and daughters will prophesy, your young men will see visions, your old men will dream dreams.❜
> *(Acts 2: 17)*

Those who don't would argue that God only sent visions to biblical prophets and apostles for a particular time and purpose.

Catholic Christians	For Catholics, the content of visions can only be accepted if they do not contradict anything taught by the Church. If the Church recognises a vision, Catholics have permission to believe what the vision reveals, but they are not required to believe that the vision is genuine. These accepted visions are rare, but Catholics do accept that God may reveal himself.
Protestant Christians	Charismatic churches, including some Anglican churches, encourage people to ask God for visions and expect him to reveal himself. Christians who experience visions are encouraged to share them with a church leader who will help them to interpret it using the Bible. Other Protestant churches, for example more conservative Anglican churches, do not accept visions and would say that God does not need to speak in any other way than through the Bible.

BUILD YOUR SKILLS

1 In your own words, describe the following:
   a what a vision is and why visions are important to Christians.
   b an account of a biblical vision.
   c an account of a non-biblical vision.

2 Finish these two sentences, making sure that you explain your reasons.
   • Visions might lead people to believe in God because...
   • Visions might lead people to reject God's existence because...

3 Why do Christians disagree about visions? Write a paragraph explaining, referring to at least two divergent Christian views. **STRETCH**

SUMMARY

• Believers think that God may reveal himself through visions.

• The sites of many visions have become places of pilgrimage and worship.

• Although many Christians believe that visions prove the existence of God, they do not always lead to belief.

C Thousands of people visit the shrine of Our Lady of Lourdes every year in the hope of being cured

EXAM-STYLE QUESTIONS

a Outline **three** things that visions show about the nature of God. (3)

d 'Visions are just hallucinations or wishful thinking.'
Evaluate this statement considering arguments for and against. In your response you should:
   • refer to Christian teachings
   • refer to non-religious points of view
   • reach a justified conclusion. (12)

What are miracles?

Miracles are amazing or impossible events which are understood to be God intervening in human life. The events bring about good, and Christians believe they can only be explained with reference to God. Many people throughout history have claimed to witness miracles, and claims of miracles are still made today.

... are an act of God and prove his existence

A

... are signs of the power and love of God

Many Christians believe miracles...

... give them hope and strengthen their faith in God

Biblical examples of miracles

In the Bible, God reveals himself to his people through miracles. One of the most famous miracles in the Old Testament is when God parts the waters of the Red Sea to allow Moses and his people to escape from Egypt.

> ❛The Lord drove the sea back with a strong east wind and turned it into dry land. The waters were divided, and the Israelites went through the sea on dry ground, with a wall of water on their right and on their left. ❜
> *(Exodus 14: 21–22)*

The miracles of Jesus

In the New Testament, Jesus performed many miracles which demonstrated his divine nature. His miracles can be categorised as follows:

- **Healing the sick**: for example, healing an official's son *(John 4: 43–54)*.
- **Overturning the laws of nature:** for example, raising Lazarus from the dead *(John 11: 17–44)*, or walking on the water *(Matthew 14: 22–33)*.
- **Casting out the forces of evil:** casting out (exorcising) an evil spirit from a young man *(Mark 9: 25–26)*.

B In Exodus, God parts the Red Sea

> ❛Jesus called in a loud voice, "Lazarus, come out!" The dead man came out, his hands and feet wrapped with strips of linen, and a cloth around his face.❜
> *(John 11: 43–44)*

Sometimes, Jesus expressed concern at people's lack of faith. At times, it seemed that all they wanted was for him to perform miracles, when Jesus wanted them to listen to his teachings and believe. When a royal official asked Jesus to cure his son, Jesus replied:

> ❛"Unless you people see signs and wonders," Jesus told him, "you will never believe."❜
> *(John 4: 48)*

According to Jesus, miracles are 'signs' of God's Kingdom, and they demonstrate the power and nature of God. They also reveal something about how Jesus relates to the Father:

> ❛The works I do in my Father's name testify about me […] even though you do not believe me, believe the works, that you may know and understand that the Father is in me, and I in the Father.❜
> *(John 10: 25, 38)*

C According to the Gospel of John, Jesus raised Lazarus from the dead

> When someone **testifies** about something, they give evidence. Jesus is saying that his miracles give evidence that proves he is the Son of God.
>
> **SUPPORT**

Do miracles lead to belief?

The non-religous viewpoint

- There might be other explanations for a miracle, such as coincidence or a very unusual event. Even if the probability is very low, unusual things do still occur.
- Scientific and medical knowledge is always developing. Humanists would argue that, just because something cannot be explained now, it does not mean that it will always be unexplainable.
- An atheist would argue that, even if something is unexplainable, it does not necessarily mean that it is caused by God or proof that God exists.

The Christian viewpoint

- There are many recorded examples of miracles in the Bible and throughout history.
- Those who experience miracles may feel that they have had direct contact with God. Christians could argue that it's very unlikely that every person who has ever claimed to experience a miracle has been mistaken.
- It could be argued that, if there is no reasonable explanation for an event, it must be supernatural, and therefore evidence of God at work.

Divergent understandings about miracles

Christians believe that the miracles described in the Bible show how omnipotent God is because he can perform acts that require unexplainable power. In addition, healing miracles show how much God loves people.

However, there are differences within Christianity in how miracles are interpreted today. These differences are mainly due to whether a Christian has a conservative or liberal viewpoint on miracles. A more liberal viewpoint would be that miracles in the Bible are powerful stories that teach about the nature of God, but that they did not actually occur (or that what happened was not a miracle but has some other natural explanation) – or that only certain miracles occurred, like Jesus rising from the dead. However, liberal Christians would argue that their lack of belief in miracles does not detract from their belief in the message and teachings of Jesus, which they believe is what really matters.

A more conservative Christian might hold a 'literalist' viewpoint and believe that all miracles in the Bible happened exactly as they are described. Other non-literalist conservative Christians could argue that it is difficult to interpret miracles in the Bible since our cultural contexts are so different. However, miracles seem so central to Jesus' life and message that their occurrence cannot be ruled out – especially miracles like the resurrection. These Christians would argue that the question of whether the miracle happened exactly as described or not is less important than their meaning and significance in interpreting who Jesus is and what this means for Christians today.

D This 25-year-old man was trapped for 11 days in rubble after an earthquake in Haiti. If you were rescued after such a long time, would you think it was a miracle you were saved? Why/why not?

BUILD YOUR SKILLS

1   In your own words, explain what a Christian understands a miracle to be.

2   a   List three examples of miracles from the Bible.
    b   What would a believer say each one shows about the nature of God?
    c   Is there another explanation for these events?

3   Read the full story of Jesus healing the official's son *(John 4: 43–54)*. What does this event tell Christians about what God is like? What would a non-religious person argue?

4   If God performs some miracles, why does he not do more to make the world a better place? How would a Christian answer?   **STRETCH**

SUMMARY

- Miracles are amazing or impossible events which are understood to be God intervening in human life.

- There are accounts in the Bible of God performing miracles.

- Many Christians believe that miracles prove the existence of God and show his love and omnipotence.

- Other people say that miracles do not prove that God exists.

EXAM-STYLE QUESTIONS

b   Explain **two** reasons why some people doubt that miracles really happen. (4)

c   Explain **two** reasons why miracles are important for Christians. In your answer you must refer to a source of wisdom and authority. (5)

What are religious experiences?

Religious experiences are events that people believe have brought them into direct contact with God, filling them with awe and sometimes fear. This may be through:

- dreams
- seeing visions (like St Bernadette; see 2.2)
- hearing God's voice
- having a **near-death experience**
- experiencing miracles (see 2.3).

Many religious experiences happen in private, but they can also involve other people.

Charismatic experiences

This type of experience usually takes place amongst a group of Christians when they worship together, as within the Charismatic and Pentecostal Churches. They believe that the experience is the result of the power and work of the Holy Spirit. The experience may take different forms, such as:

- speaking in tongues (a divine language unknown to the speaker)
- making prophecies about the future
- speaking words of wisdom
- healing others through the power of God.

Near-death experiences

This type of experience can happen when a person is very close to death or has technically died, for example, during an operation. When they recover, some people recall having an experience that they cannot explain. If they felt God's presence, Christians would call it a religious experience. Other people experience things like passing through a tunnel of light or seeing loved ones who have died. Christians would say this was a spiritual rather than a religious experience because it did not involve God. Experiences like this are very intense and may cause the person to reflect on their life and make changes.

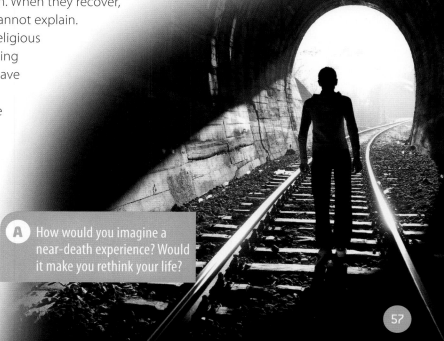

> **SPECIFICATION FOCUS**
>
> **Christian attitudes towards religious experiences and its use as a philosophical argument for the existence of God:** the nature of a religious experience and why it might be regarded as revelation including reference to Exodus 3; Christian responses to non-religious (including atheist and Humanist) arguments that religious experiences do not provide proof that God exists.

> **USEFUL TERMS**
>
> **Near-death experience:** an experience when someone who later revives is close to death
>
> **Religious experience:** an event that a person believes has brought them in direct contact with God

> **SUPPORT**
>
> Do you think that near-death experiences are real? If not, how could they be explained?

A How would you imagine a near-death experience? Would it make you rethink your life?

57

Are religious experiences revelations?

Many Christians who have had a religious experience may feel that they have had a revelation, in which God revealed his greatness, holiness, and/or loving nature.

After the experience, the person might feel that they understand the nature of God more clearly or feel reassured by the presence of God in their life. They may feel that the experience has helped them to see a way through the difficulties in their life more clearly. They may feel that God answered specific prayers or showed them a better way to live their lives. Such an experience may convince the person to convert to Christianity or to try to live a better life. Religious experiences affect people in different ways, but may change lives dramatically.

Biblical revelation: Moses' religious experience

In the book of Exodus, Moses had a dramatic religious experience which Christians regard as a revelation. He was shepherding a flock when he saw a bush that was on fire, but it was not burning up. He went to look:

> ❛When the Lord saw that he had gone over to look, **God called to him from within the bush**, "Moses! Moses!" And Moses said, "Here I am." "Do not come any closer," God said. "Take off your sandals, for the place where you are standing is holy ground." Then he said, "**I am the God of your father**, the God of Abraham, the God of Isaac and the God of Jacob." At this, Moses hid his face, because he was afraid to look at God.❜
> *(Exodus 3: 4–6)*

According to the Bible, this encounter changed Moses' life and the lives of many others: he was called by God to rescue his people from slavery in Egypt.

B Christians believe that Jesus was the final, complete revelation

C Moses' religious experience was a revelation from God

Do religious experiences prove God exists?

Non-religious people could argue that religious experiences do not prove that God exists for any of the following reasons.

Non-religious arguments	Christian responses
There is a lack of scientific evidence for religious experiences. Humanists believe that science is the only reliable source of evidence about the world.	Science itself was created by God, and is therefore only useful to a certain extent. God can still choose to act outside of science.
There could be other explanations for the events, such as the imagination, or hallucinations caused by ill-health, drugs, or alcohol.	Religious experiences are sometimes witnessed and are often 'weighed up' by a third party.
Religious experiences could be a form of 'wish fulfilment'. This is the idea that a person might believe an event happened simply because they have a very strong desire for it to be true.	Christians are looking for a genuine experience of God. They could argue that genuine religious experiences are clearly not generated by themselves.

BUILD YOUR SKILLS

1 Explain what a Christian may understand as a religious experience.

2 List the following 'religious experiences' in order, from the most convincing (1) to the least convincing (6). Explain your order.

'In the earthquake, the building I was in fell down and I was the only survivor.'

'I asked God to speak to me and he whispered to me to pray for the poor.'

'We were all praising God in a large crowd, when suddenly the Virgin Mary appeared and spoke to us. We all saw her!'

'I visited a religious faith-healer who prayed for me and my illness was cured.'

'I asked God to help me in the exam – and all the questions were easy.'

'I asked God to strengthen my faith in him – and he did.'

3 Create a revision mind-map which gives reasons for and against religious experiences as proof that God exists.

D A modern crime scene can be tested in many different ways. Can religious experiences be tested?

SUMMARY

- Religious experiences take various forms and take place in different situations.
- Some people think such experiences come from God, but others think there are very different explanations.
- Religious experiences can convert people to Christianity or give them a stronger faith in God.

EXAM-STYLE QUESTIONS

a Outline **three** features of religious experiences. (3)

c Explain **two** reasons why religious experiences might help some people to believe in God. In your answer you must refer to a source of wisdom and authority. (5)

Christian teaching about prayers

What is prayer?

Prayer is a way of communicating with God, usually (but not always) through words. Prayer is of fundamental importance to the Christian life, because it's the way that Christians communicate with the God they worship and establish a personal relationship with him. For Christians, answered prayers are often seen as confirmation that God is listening and cares for them.

Prayer can take place privately or with others, and can include praising God for who he is, asking God to help others, repenting of sin, and so on. You can read more about specific kinds of prayer in unit 3.3.

What does the Bible teach about prayer?

The Bible teaches that God hears and answers the prayers of faithful people.

> ❛This is the confidence we have in approaching God: that **if we ask anything according to his will, he hears us**. And if we know that he hears us – whatever we ask – we know that we have what we asked of him.❜
> *(1 John 5: 14–15)*

> ❛Is anyone among you sick? [...] the prayer offered in faith will make the sick person well [...] pray for each other that you may be healed. **The prayer of a righteous person is powerful and effective.**❜
> *(James 5: 14–16)*

> ❛You may ask me for anything in my name, and I will do it.❜
> *(Jesus speaking in John 14: 14)*

These teachings say that:

- Christians should be 'confident' in approaching God and that he will listen
- Christians should try to pray according to God's will – i.e. pray about matters that are in-keeping with God's plans for people and the world
- Christians should pray for themselves and others to be healed from sickness.

SPECIFICATION FOCUS

Christian teaching about prayers: Christian teachings about the nature and importance of prayers; Christian teachings about reasons prayers that are answered in the way the person expects might lead to belief in God, including 1 John 5: 13–17.

SUPPORT

According to this quotation, why might God choose not to answer certain prayers?

STRETCH

Christians often say 'in Jesus' name, Amen' at the end of prayers. What do you think it means to ask for something 'in the name of Jesus'? What difference do you think this would make to the nature of the prayer?

 Prayer can take place privately or with others

Do answered prayers lead to belief in God?

If God answers a prayer in the way the person who prays expects, it is very likely to make them believe in him or to strengthen their existing faith. To them, it proves that God is listening and cares about them. It also reinforces teachings in the Bible, which say that God rewards those who are faithful.

Not all prayers appear to be answered. Christians believe that God may answer a prayer in an unexpected way, perhaps because he acts in their best interests. When they realise what has happened, it may still strengthen their faith.

Christians also believe that God may answer a request with a 'No', or may not answer at all. Though this can sometimes challenge a believer's faith, Christians believe that God is wise and trust that he has their best interests at heart.

USEFUL TERMS

Prayer: a way of communicating with God

CASE STUDY: WORLD WAR I

In April 1915, British soldiers fighting in World War I were in great danger under heavy gunfire. They prayed to God to help them and many men claim they saw an angel, which led them to safety. This incident was reported in newspapers all over the world and the figure was named the Angel of Mons.

Arthur Barraclough, a soldier fighting during the same war, died in 2004 aged 106. He attributed his survival to prayer:

SUPPORT

Do you think either of these examples are answered prayers? Explain your ideas.

> ❝I always said a prayer before going over the top… I'll never forget it. "Dear God, I am going into grave danger. Please help me to act like a man and come back safe." And that's what I did. And I went over without fear. That little prayer seemed to save my life because I had no fear left… And six times I went up and six times I said that little prayer and each time I went up and come back safe. And I thank God for it every time. ❞

STRETCH

'If God was all-loving, he would have saved all of the soldiers in WWI, not just the ones who prayed.' Consider whether you agree or disagree with this statement and explain why.

B

BUILD YOUR SKILLS

1   Reread the Bible quotations on page 60. Using your own words, write a short paragraph on what Christian teachings say about prayers.

2   a   Read the account from Arthur Barraclough.

    b   What impact did answered prayer have on his faith in God?

3   Look at image **C**. If God exists, why doesn't he answer prayers for suffering like this to end? Write an answer to this question, including a Christian perspective, and your own conclusions.   **STRETCH**

C   People queue for food after flooding in Pakistan

SUMMARY

- The Bible teaches that God will answer the prayers of those who believe in him.
- Christians regard answered prayer as confirmation that God exists.

? EXAM-STYLE QUESTIONS

a   Outline **three** reasons why Christians pray. (3)

c   Explain **two** reasons why Christians think that answered prayers lead to belief in God. In your answer you must refer to a source of wisdom and authority. (5)

2.6 Design argument

What is the design argument?

The **design argument** is an argument for the existence of God. It suggests that because so much of nature appears to be ordered and purposeful, it must have been designed, and this designer is God. It is found in many different **philosophy** and belief systems. The earliest recorded versions come from ancient Greece and Rome.

SPECIFICATION FOCUS

Design argument: the classical design argument for the existence of God and its use by Christians as a philosophical argument for the existence of God; divergent understandings about what the design argument may show about the nature of God for Christians including Romans 1: 18–24; Christian responses to non-religious (including atheist and Humanist) arguments against the design argument as evidence for the existence of God.

Thomas Aquinas

In the thirteenth century, the famous Catholic thinker St Thomas Aquinas (1225–1274) wrote about 'Five Ways' to prove the existence of God. The design argument was one of these ways. He argued that even plants, which don't have knowledge, are ordered and have purpose. He claimed this could not happen by chance, therefore it makes sense to assume they are directed to act in this way by an intelligent designer.

USEFUL TERMS

Design argument: the argument that God must exist because the universe is so complex, purposeful, and beautiful that it had to be created by an intelligent being

Philosophy: the study of the truths about life, morals, etc.

A Thomas Aquinas said that an arrow does not know where to aim; only the archer gives it direction or purpose

William Paley

In his book *Natural Theology*, Anglican vicar William Paley (1743–1805) made a comparison between a watch and the universe. If you look at a watch, you would not assume the parts had come together by chance. It has many complex and distinctive parts that work together for a purpose. He believed that, in the same way, we cannot assume that the order of the universe is accidental – it must have been designed with a purpose.

B This watch is just 6 cm in diameter, works 'like clockwork', and looks intricately beautiful

How would Christians use the design argument?

Many Christians believe that because the universe is so well ordered and beautiful it must have been designed by God, and therefore God exists:

- Everything in the universe is very complex and appears to have been designed for a purpose. The evidence is in what we can see, hear, smell, taste, and touch.
- All the parts had to be put together in the right way, and to go on working in the right way, for them to fulfil that purpose. That could not just happen by chance.
- The beauty of the universe does not always seem to serve a practical purpose, so this also suggests a loving God who wants to make the universe beautiful.
- Only an omnipotent being such as God could create a universe so complex and beautiful.

Divergent understandings about the design argument

Christians believe that God reveals his nature clearly in creation. In the book of Romans, the following passage says that, therefore, all people should see this and believe:

> ❛For since the creation of the world God's invisible qualities – his eternal power and divine nature – **have been clearly seen**, being understood from what has been made, **so that people are without excuse**.❜
> *(Romans 1: 20)*

In other words, if people have seen the beauty of creation, they have seen God, and therefore have no excuse for not believing in him.

Some Christians might use this as an argument for why non-believers will be judged by God for their unbelief (see 1.6) – they have 'no excuse' for not following God because of what they can see and experience of him in the world. Other Christians would argue that the world is not necessarily enough to bring about belief, and that many people need to be told about God in order to believe in him (see 3.6).

There are many things in nature like this that seem **SUPPORT** ordered and beautiful. Can you think of more examples?

USEFUL TERMS

Analogy: a comparison between two things that have similarities

C A wildfire. If God designed the natural world, why do events like these naturally occur?

What is the evidence against the design argument?

Non-religious people could argue that the design argument does not prove that God exists for any of the following reasons:

Non-religious arguments	Christian responses
The universe is unique so we cannot use an **analogy** to explain it, as argued by David Hume (1711–1776).	Analogies can help humans to consider complex and mysterious ideas, for example the supreme power and love of God.
The universe is not perfect. If God designed it, why does he allow things that seem to be disastrous, like disease, evil, and natural disasters?	Suffering was not part of God's original design: it has existed since the Fall. God will one day bring an end to all suffering (see 1.7–1.8).
The universe may not be ordered and purposeful. Richard Dawkins (1941–) suggests that people see the world with 'purpose coloured spectacles'. They only see order because they look for it.	Order can be observed because it is present; the universe shows evidence of complex processes which have a purpose, e.g. the water cycle, the human body.
Since Charles Darwin (1809–1882) proposed the theory of evolution, most people believe that living things evolve through natural selection, which happens by chance rather than by design.	Evolution and natural selection can also be considered to be complex processes which are part of God's design.

BUILD YOUR SKILLS

1 In your own words, write an explanation of the design argument.

2 The scientist Isaac Newton (1643–1727) realised that every human being has a unique thumbprint. This convinced him of the existence of an intelligent designer of the world. Do you find this to be a convincing argument? Explain your reasons.

? EXAM-STYLE QUESTIONS

a Outline **three** things that the classical design argument shows about the nature of God for Christians. (3)

d 'The classical design argument proves the existence of God.' Evaluate this statement considering arguments for and against. In your response you should:
  • refer to Christian teachings
  • refer to non-religous points of view
  • reach a justified conclusion. (12)

SUMMARY

• Many believers argue that its order, purpose, and beauty suggest that the universe must have been created by an intelligent being – God.

• Critics of this design argument say that it fails to prove that God exists because the universe may not be designed at all.

2.7 Cosmological argument

What is the cosmological argument?

The **cosmological argument** is an argument for the existence of God. It suggests that something must have happened to 'start' the universe (known as a **prime mover**). The key claims of the cosmological argument are as follows:

- Cause and effect are key features of our world. Everything within it exists because it was caused by something else.
- The very existence of the universe requires an explanation or first cause. Without a first cause, the chain of cause and effect would stretch infinitely backwards, which seems impossible.
- God is this first cause of the universe.

What does the cosmological argument show about the nature of God?

Christians believe that the cosmological argument shows the omnipotent nature of God. As the first cause, God has the power to create all things in the universe from nothing. Therefore his power is limitless.

Christians also believe that, unlike all elements in the universe, God is eternal. He has always existed, and therefore is the only being that could have created the universe.

SPECIFICATION FOCUS

Cosmological argument: the cosmological argument for the existence of God and its use by Christians as a philosophical argument for the existence of God; divergent understandings about what the cosmological argument shows about the nature of God for Christians, including Thomas Aquinas' First Three Ways of showing God's existence; Christian responses to non-religious (including atheist and Humanist) arguments against the cosmological argument as evidence for the existence of God.

USEFUL TERMS

Cosmological argument: an argument for the existence of God which suggests something must have started the universe

Prime mover: the first cause of all other things

A Aquinas' First Way: can the wood get hot and burn on its own?

The argument according to Aquinas

Thomas Aquinas (see 2.6) interpreted the argument in the first three of his 'Five Ways', his philosophical argument to prove the existence of God. His Three Ways can be summarised as follows:

First Way: the unmoved mover

- We can see that some things in the world are 'in motion', that is they change.
- Nothing can move/change by itself, so everything has to be moved by something else that is in motion.
- This chain of movers must have a beginning otherwise nothing would ever have started moving.
- There must be a first unmoved mover that causes the motion in all things.
- We understand that first mover to be God.

Aquinas' example was a fire (which is *actually* hot) as the cause of wood (which is *potentially* hot) changing to a state of being actually hot. When something changes it is because something else has caused it to change.

Second Way: the first cause

- We can see that everything has a cause.
- Nothing can cause itself, so everything has to be caused by something else.
- This chain of causes must have a beginning otherwise nothing would ever be caused. If there was no first cause, there could be no intermediate causes and no final cause.
- There must be a first cause on which all causes depend.
- We call that first cause God.

Third Way: possibility and necessity

- We can see that everything in the world exists for a time and then does not exist.
- Those things cannot always exist because, if there is a possibility that they will not exist, then at some time they will not exist.
- If it is possible for everything to not exist, then at some time nothing existed.
- However if there was a time when nothing existed, then nothing would exist now, which is clearly not the case.
- Therefore, some things are not merely possible, but must exist because they are necessary.
- Every necessary thing is caused by something else, but this chain of causes must have a beginning otherwise nothing would ever be caused.
- We must conclude that there is something that is necessary in itself and we call this God.

> ‘Now in efficient causes it is not possible to go on [back] to infinity […] therefore **it is necessary to admit a first cause, to which everyone gives the name God.**’
> (St Thomas Aquinas)

> Could anything other than fire cause the wood to change? Does it make sense to say that nothing caused the wood to change? **SUPPORT**

B Each domino causes the next domino to fall. What caused the first one to fall?

What is the evidence against the cosmological argument?

Non-religious people could argue that the cosmological argument does not prove that God exists for any of the following reasons:

Non-religious arguments	Christian responses
Bertrand Russell (1872–1970), a famous atheist who was also involved with the British Humanist Association, said that just because everything within the universe needs a cause, it does not mean that the universe as a whole needs a cause.	Thomas Aquinas argues in his Second Way that the chain of causes must have a beginning otherwise nothing would ever have been caused.
David Hume (1711–1776), widely believed to have been an atheist, argued that there is nothing wrong with saying that things can come into existence without a cause.	The universe could not have come about by chance. As described in the Bible, God was the first cause of the universe.
Even if there does logically need to be a first cause, why does that cause need to be God?	God is the supreme designer, who is by nature eternal and uncreated. There is no other being like God.
Modern scientists argue that the universe caused itself in the Big Bang. If 'God' doesn't need a first cause, then why does the universe need a first cause?	God could have caused the Big Bang. God is eternal and therefore cannot be compared with elements within the universe.

BUILD YOUR SKILLS

1   Write an explanation of the cosmological argument. Try to use an analogy, for example dominoes (see image **B**).

2   a   Copy and complete the following table, using the information in this unit and your own ideas.

Cosmological argument	
Strengths	**Weaknesses**

   b   Are you more convinced by the strengths or by the weaknesses? Why? Write a short paragraph explaining your reasons.

SUMMARY

- Many believers argue that the existence of the universe supports belief in God because everything that exists must have a cause and God is the most likely cause.

- Critics suggest that there is no need to find an explanation for everything, and even if there was, God is not the only possible or even the most likely explanation.

C Did the universe cause itself?

EXAM-STYLE QUESTIONS

b   Explain **two** reasons why a non-religious person might argue against the cosmological argument as proof of the existence of God. (4)

d   'The cosmological argument proves the existence of God.' Evaluate this statement considering arguments for and against. In your response you should:
   - refer to Christian teachings
   - refer to non-religious points of view
   - reach a justified conclusion. (12)

2.8 Religious upbringing

SPECIFICATION FOCUS

Religious upbringing: Christian teachings about raising children to believe in God, including reference to Proverbs 22: 6; features of a Christian upbringing and why they may lead to belief in God; Christian responses to non-religious (including atheist and Humanist) arguments about why a religious upbringing may result in a rejection of God's existence.

Christian teachings about religious upbringing

The Bible says that the effort made by parents while bringing up a child is likely to impact that child for the rest of his or her life:

> ❛Start children off on the way they should go, and even when they are old they will not turn from it.❜
> *(Proverbs 22: 6)*

The *Catechism of the Catholic Church* also teaches that there is a role for the whole family in a child's upbringing:

> ❛The family is the community in which, from childhood, one can learn moral values, begin to honour God and make good use of freedom.❜
> *(CCC 2207)*

SUPPORT This means that the family can teach about good and bad behaviour, worshipping God, and making wise choices throughout life.

Christian teachings like these are why Christian parents teach their children about God and bring them up in the Christian faith. When a child is old enough, most Christians would encourage their child to make a decision for themselves about the Christian faith.

What are the features of a Christian upbringing?

Faith is an important part of a Christian family's life together. Christian parents want their children to develop the same faith as their own, so that each child comes to know God and receives everlasting life through him. There are various ways that Christian parents can encourage their children's belief in God. At home, they can:

- teach children how to pray to God and thank him for the good things in life
- show children how to live a Christian life by following Christian teachings
- introduce children to the Bible's teachings and explain their significance
- celebrate Christian festivals together and explain their significance to children.

Christian families do not have to be alone in providing a Christian upbringing for their children. They are part of a wider Christian community, represented locally by the local parish church or chapel with the same faith, values, and religious practices.

In the Catholic, Orthodox, and Anglican Churches, families introduce their children to the Christian faith by having them baptised. This ceremony welcomes a child into the Christian community. During the **baptism** service, water is poured on the child's head to demonstrate that their sins are washed away at the start of their Christian life.

The Church community then shares the responsibility of encouraging children to believe in God. They do this by:

- providing a wider community and other Christian role models for children to follow
- running Sunday School, where children learn about Christian teachings and how to put them into living practice
- encouraging children to attend church services with their parents or as part of Sunday School
- running Bible study groups and prayer groups that children can join
- putting on special events such as church fairs that encourage children to enjoy being in the Church community.

When a child or young person decides for themself that they want to become a full member of the Church, they attend Bible study classes and are then confirmed. The Catholic **confirmation** service can happen shortly after a child is 8 years old, but in some Catholic churches children wait until they are older. In the Anglican Church, children are usually confirmed between the ages of 12 and 15.

USEFUL TERMS

Baptism: the Christian ceremony that welcomes a person into the Christian community

Confirmation: the Christian ceremony that accepts a person who formally asks to become a member of the Church

A A Catholic confirmation service

Why might a Christian upbringing lead to belief in God?

A Christian upbringing could lead to belief in God for the following reasons:

- Young children naturally copy what their parents say and do. If their parents and wider community tell them that God exists, they are likely to believe it.
- Children who are taught to pray and to believe that their prayers are heard by God are more likely to believe that God exists, especially if they believe that their prayers have been answered.
- Going to Church and attending Sunday School will involve listening to Christian teachings about God and may also involve a child experiencing God for themselves in a religious experience. This would support their belief in God.
- Many children find that being part of the Christian community brings them comfort and joy. This might establish a way of life that grows into a mature love and belief in God.

B At Sunday School, children learn about God through various activities

Why might a Christian upbringing result in a rejection of God's existence?

Sometimes it is difficult for children to continue to accept their family's religious beliefs as they grow up because:

- They learn about other beliefs and ways of life.
- They work out a different set of beliefs for themselves.
- They may have had a negative experience of religious upbringing in the family and/or in the community.
- They may choose an atheist perspective because they think there cannot be a God if there is so much suffering in the world, for example.
- They may say that science proves that Christian beliefs about God creating the world are wrong.
- They may choose a Humanist perspective because they feel it is not clear that humanity needs to worship God at all but must look after and care for itself.

Non-religious people could argue that a religious upbringing may *cause* unbelief in God:

Non-religious arguments	Christian responses
The British Humanist Association promotes children from different backgrounds mixing together. Therefore they are opposed to schooling which separates children out according to the belief of their parents. Humanists might argue that children could grow up to resent this decision that was made on their behalf.	Many Christians also promote getting to know people from other backgrounds, whether or not they school their children separately. Many encourage their children to talk about their faith and experiences openly so that any concerns can be addressed.
If a religious upbringing tells a child what to believe without inviting them to question those beliefs for themselves, then a child might become disillusioned with the faith and seek answers elsewhere.	Christians believe it is important that children should be brought up to understand the faith of their family and community. However, most Christians would agree with this non-religious view and therefore invite their children to make their own decision when they are ready to.

SUMMARY

- The Bible teaches that investing in children when they are young will teach them the right path for the rest of their lives.
- Parents can help children believe in God by giving them a Christian upbringing within the family and the wider Church community.
- As children grow up, some will maintain their belief in God but others will reject the Christian faith.

BUILD YOUR SKILLS

1 a List all the ways a child might be encouraged by their family and Church community to believe in God.
   b Which ways do you think are the most effective and which are the least effective? Explain why.

2 Does a religious upbringing always lead to belief in God? Give reasons, making sure you refer to Christian and non-religious viewpoints.

3 'No family, whether religious or non-religious, can avoid passing their beliefs on to their children.' What is your view on this statement? Explain your reasoning.

STRETCH

EXAM-STYLE QUESTIONS

a Outline **three** features of a Christian upbringing. (3)
c Explain **two** ways in which a Christian upbringing may lead to belief in God. In your answer, you must refer to a source of wisdom and authority. (5)

Revision

BUILD YOUR SKILLS

Look at the list of 'I can' statements below and think carefully about how confident you are. Use the following code to rate each of the statements. Be honest!

Green – very confident. What is your evidence for this?

Orange – quite confident. What is your target? Be specific.

Red – not confident. What is your target? Be specific.

A self-assessment revision checklist is available on *Kerboodle*

I can...

- Explain what revelation means, including reference to sources of wisdom and authority

- Explain different Christian views on what revelation shows about the nature of God

- Explain what visions are, including reference to biblical and non-biblical examples

- Give reasons why visions might lead to belief in the existence of God

- Give some non-religious arguments which maintain that visions provide no proof that God exists, and explain how Christians might respond

- Explain different Christian views on what visions show about the nature of God

- Explain what miracles are, with reference to a source of wisdom and authority

- Give reasons why miracles might lead to belief in the existence of God

- Give some non-religious arguments which maintain that miracles provide no proof that God exists, and explain how Christians might respond

- Explain different Christian views on what miracles show about the nature of God

- Explain what religious experiences are and why they might be regarded as revelation, with reference to a source of wisdom and authority

- Give some non-religious arguments which maintain that religious experiences provide no proof that God exists, and explain how Christians might respond

- Explain why prayer is important, with reference to Christian teachings

- Give reasons why answered prayers might lead people to believe in God

- Describe the design argument and explain how it might be used as an argument for the existence of God

- Explain different views on what the design argument may show about the nature of God for Christians, including reference to a source of wisdom and authority

- Give some non-religious arguments against the design argument, and explain how Christians might respond

- Describe the cosmological argument and explain how it might be used as an argument for the existence of God

- Explain different views on what the cosmological argument may show about the nature of God for Christians, including reference to a source of wisdom and authority

- Give some non-religious arguments against the cosmological argument, and explain how Christians might respond

- Give Christian teachings about raising children to believe in God

- Describe the features of a Christian upbringing and explain how they may lead to belief in God

- Give some non-religious arguments about why a religious upbringing may result in a rejection of God's existence, and explain how Christians might respond.

Exam practice

On these exam practice pages you will see example answers for each of the exam question types: **a**, **b**, **c**, and **d**. You can find out more about these on pages 6–10.

• Question 'a'

*Question **a** is AO1 – this tests your knowledge and understanding.*

> (a)   Outline **three** things that visions show about the nature of God. (3)

Student response

Visions reveal that God has plans, and they help people to change their lives. Visions show people that God loves them.

Improved student response

Visions reveal that God has plans, and they show people that God loves them. They show that God wants to communicate with his people.

   Over to you! Give yourself three minutes on the clock and have a go at answering this question. Remember, this question type requires you to provide three facts or short ideas: you don't need to explain them or express any opinions.

 WHAT WENT WELL

This student understands that visions are important and can have an effect on people's lives.

 HOW TO IMPROVE

The three things that are shown should all be about God and his nature. To make the response clearer, the student should link the points to the nature of God, not the effects of the visions on people. See the 'improved student response' opposite for a suggested correction.

• Question 'b'

*Question **b** is AO1 – this tests your knowledge and understanding.*

> (b)   Explain **two** reasons why a non-religious person might argue against the cosmological argument as proof of the existence of God. (4)

Student response

The cosmological argument states that everything has a cause, but this does not mean the universe has to have a cause. Even if the universe is caused, this does not mean that the cause has to be God.

Improved student response

The cosmological argument states that everything has a cause, but the famous atheist Bertrand Russell acknowledges that just because everything within the universe needs a cause this does not mean the universe itself also has to have a cause, therefore it could have caused itself without the need for God.

Another reason is that, even if the universe is caused, this does not mean that the cause has to be God. Modern scientists believe that the universe was a result of the Big Bang and therefore had nothing to do with God.

   Over to you! Give yourself four minutes on the clock and have a go at answering this question. Remember, in order to 'explain' something, you need to **develop** your points. See page 9 for a reminder of how to do this.

 WHAT WENT WELL

This is a mid-level response with two basic reasons given. Though the points are not developed, they are correct.

 HOW TO IMPROVE

For a high level response, students should explain why each argument is effective at disproving the cosmological argument as supporting the existence of God. See the 'improved student response' opposite for suggested corrections.

• Question 'c'

*Question **c** is A01 – this tests your knowledge and understanding.*

> (c) Explain **two** reasons why religious experiences might help some people to believe in God. In your answer you must refer to a source of wisdom and authority. (5)

Student response

God can choose to do what he wants because he is omnipotent. Religious experiences prove God exists because people see them and believe.

Improved student response

Science can only explain so much. Because it is limited in its understanding, God can choose to act outside of the realms of science and this may help someone to believe in him.

Christians are looking for a genuine experience of God, like Moses' experience in the Bible where 'God called to him from within the bush' (Exodus 3: 4). Christians could argue that these experiences are not generated by themselves and further their understanding and belief in God.

 Over to you! Give yourself five minutes on the clock and have a go at answering this question. Remember, you need to write two developed points, one of which needs to be supported by a source of wisdom and authority.

 WHAT WENT WELL

This student understands that religious experiences can lead to belief in God and often cannot be explained.

 HOW TO IMPROVE

The link between the religious experience and how it causes belief in God could be clearer. Has the student included a source of wisdom and authority? See the 'improved student response' opposite for suggested corrections.

• Question 'd'

*Question **d** is A02 – this tests your ability to evaluate.*

> (d) 'The classical design argument proves the existence of God.' Evaluate this statement considering arguments for and against. In your response you should:
> • refer to Christian teachings
> • refer to non-religious points of view
> • reach a justified conclusion. (12)

Student response

I agree the design argument proves the existence of God because it suggests that so much of nature appears to be ordered and purposeful, it must have been designed and the only designer powerful enough is God.

An atheist will argue against this, suggesting that there are examples of natural evil within the universe, therefore if it was designed by God would he have created disasters and disease?

To conclude the design argument proves that God exists and designed the universe because there is so much evidence of complex and beautiful things.

 WHAT WENT WELL

This is a low level response. The student understands that they must give two opposing sides of the argument and reach a conclusion. They explain briefly both arguments and present their initial argument as a conclusion.

Improved student response

I agree the design argument proves the existence of God because it is one of the 'five ways' Catholic St. Thomas Aquinas wrote to prove the existence of God (1225–1274). For centuries the design argument has been used to explain how so much of nature appears to be ordered and purposeful, the conclusion being that it must have been designed and the only designer powerful enough is God.

This was supported by William Paley (1743–1805) in his book 'Natural Theology' where he makes a comparison between a watch and the universe. As the parts of a watch are purposeful and well-designed, so are aspects of the universe. Paley argues you would not assume a watch had happened by chance and neither has the universe. God, omnipotent and omniscient, is responsible for the design of the world.

However, an atheist, such as Richard Dawkins, will argue against this, suggesting that the universe may not be ordered and purposeful and because we look for examples of order we can find them. Other arguments suggest that God could not be responsible for the design of the universe because there are examples of natural evil within the universe and that could not be a product of an omnipotent and benevolent God.

To conclude I still agree that the design argument proves the existence of God because there is so much evidence of complexity and design within the world that it could not have come about by chance. In addition, God reveals to Christians his nature through creation: 'For since the creation of the world God's invisible qualities – his eternal power and divine nature – have been clearly seen' (Romans 1: 20), meaning that if you have seen the beauty of creation, you have seen God and have no reason not to believe.

Over to you! Give yourself 12 minutes on the clock and have a go at answering this question. Remember to refer back to the original statement in your writing when you give different points of view, and make sure you cover each of the bullet points given in the question.

! HOW TO IMPROVE

Both sides of the argument lack detailed understanding. Has the student included a source of wisdom and authority? See the 'improved student response' opposite for suggested corrections.

BUILD YOUR SKILLS

In your exams, you'll need to make sure you use religious terminology correctly. Do you know the meaning of the following important terms for this topic?

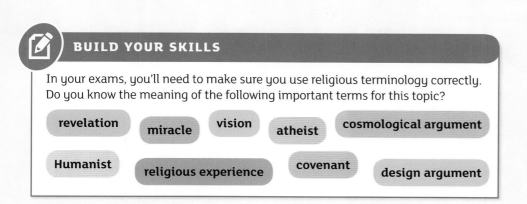

- revelation
- miracle
- vision
- atheist
- cosmological argument
- Humanist
- religious experience
- covenant
- design argument

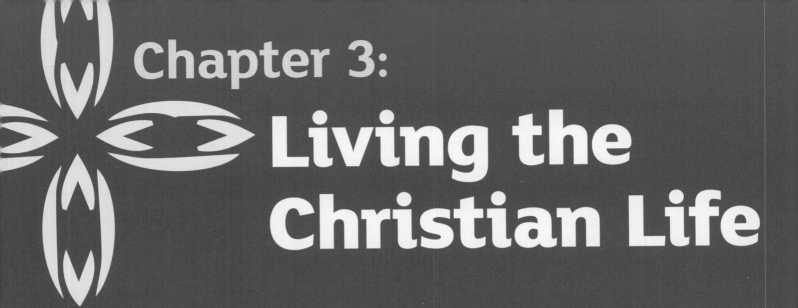

Chapter 3:
Living the Christian Life

SPECIFICATION FOCUS

Christian worship: liturgical and non-liturgical forms of worship, including activities which are informal and individual, including reference to the Book of Common Prayer; when each form might be used and why; divergent Christian attitudes towards the practices, meaning and significance of liturgical and non-liturgical forms of worship in Christian life today, with reference to denominations who worship with less structure such as some Pentecostal churches.

Living the Christian life is a decision on the part of an individual to live as a follower of Jesus. This chapter looks at the various activities that these followers take part in. Although these activities have strong similarities, there are clearly different emphases and divergent attitudes represented between different Christian **denominations**. These differences are often clearest between denominations, but this is not always the case, and it is worth noting that the larger denominations (for instance Anglicans and Catholics) often have a wide range of styles represented within the same denomination.

Worship is when religious believers express their love and respect for and devotion to God. It is a time when Christians can thank God, ask his forgiveness and pray for themselves, other people and the world at large. It helps them to feel closer to God.

Liturgical and non-liturgical worship

Christians can worship in different ways:

- **liturgical worship**: usually following an agreed form of words (often the congregation follow the words in a service book or on an overhead screen).
- **non-liturgical worship**: although the service will have a clear structure, there will be no, or very few, set words other than the words to songs.
- individual worship: quiet worship alone in a person's own home.

The Anglican Church has both liturgical and non-liturgical services. An Anglican service from the *Book of Common Prayer* or the more recent service book *Common Worship* will contain set services. The text in ordinary type indicates when the priest or service leader will read, and the text in bold type indicates when everyone should read together. Here is an example from an Anglican communion service:

	The Lord be with you
All	**and also with you.**
	Lift up your hearts.
All	**We lift them to the Lord.**
	Let us give thanks to the Lord our God.
All	**It is right to give thanks and praise.**

It is right to praise you, Father, Lord of all creation;
in your love you made us for yourself.

When we turned away
you did not reject us,
but came to meet us in your Son.

All **You embraced us as your children**
and welcomed us to sit and eat with you.

A The Anglican communion service is an example of liturgical worship

B Various denominations use modern styles of worship in both liturgical and non-liturgical services

STRETCH

Music is an important feature of liturgical and non-liturgical worship. It is used to praise and express belief in God. Find out what types of music are used in worship and the titles of some specific pieces. Why do you think music like this is so important to worshippers?

Methodists and Catholics will have similar service books. The Anglican denomination also has an informal, non-liturgical service. The structure of that service will usually follow a pattern of prayer, sung worship, Bible reading and a **sermon**.

There is very little prescription as to what prayers are said or what songs are sung. This style of service might also be found in a Catholic church, but would be more common in Baptist and Pentecostal Churches. There would, however, be considerable stylistic differences in the sung worship elements of each of those services. The instruments would also vary from organ music, which might be more familiar in a Methodist or Baptist setting, to brass bands in a Salvation Army setting, to electric guitars and drums in a Pentecostal setting. By this point in the 21st Century however, all styles of instrument and worship could be found in all denominations.

The Book of Common Prayer

The *Book of Common Prayer* (BCP) is the oldest Anglican service book. It was written in the sixteenth century by Thomas Cranmer, and modified in 1662. Many of its prayers and services are still used today. The BCP also contains the special services for ordaining Priests and Bishops, baptism, wedding and funeral services, the **creeds**, the 39 Articles (see 3.2), and special prayers for each week of the year. Here is a prayer from the BCP that has been prayed since the 17th Century:

> ❛Lighten our darkness, we beseech thee, O Lord;
> and by thy great mercy defend us from
> all perils and dangers of this night;
> for the love of thy only Son, our Saviour, Jesus Christ.
> Amen. ❜
> *From the Book of Common Prayer*

Divergent Christian attitudes

As we have seen, liturgical and non-liturgical forms of worship occur in various different denominations, and most Christians will worship using both forms. However, some Christians will prefer one over the other. For example, Christians who value liturgical worship find comfort in using words that may well have been

USEFUL TERMS

Creed: a statement of firmly held beliefs; for example, the Apostles' Creed or the Nicene Creed

Denominations: the name given to the main groups within the Church

Liturgical: a set form of worship, usually following agreed words

Non-liturgical: a form of worship which is not set

Sermon: a talk or teaching from a church leader

Worship: believers expressing love and respect for, and devotion to, God

said for decades, or, in the case of the *Book of Common Prayer*, for centuries. There is also some security in knowing exactly the pattern the service will follow, the length of time it will take, and usually that the form of words used have been authorised by a particular denominational hierarchy.

The non-liturgical service pattern is far more common in Charismatic Churches, such as Pentecostal Churches and an increasing number of Anglican Churches, and in these churches the emphasis is placed on 'following the Spirit'; in other words, listening to God and following his lead in worship. Christians who value non-liturgical worship tend to appreciate the fact that they have more freedom to express their worship – this might involve lifting hands or even dancing. Typically the sung worship may be of any length, the service may or may not have structured prayers, the service leader has far more control of the service and is able to weave in different aspects, for example a video clip or group discussion. Elements of the service can change during the service, extra songs can be added, or an extended prayer time can be introduced.

Individual worship

Believers often worship God on their own. They may want to praise God for who he is, or so that they can feel closer to him, or they may have a particular problem they want to talk to God about. Individual worship can include prayer, meditation, Bible reading, singing and quiet thinking.

 BUILD YOUR SKILLS

1 Copy and complete the following table for the main ideas about Christian worship in this unit. The first type of worship has been given for you.

Type of worship	What does it involve?	Why is it important for Christians?
Liturgical worship		

2 What is the *Book of Common Prayer* and why is it important to some Christians? Write a short paragraph of explanation.

3 Why might some Christians prefer either liturgical or non-liturgical worship? Try to refer to at least one denomination in your answer.

 COMPARE AND CONTRAST

In your exam, you could be asked to **compare and contrast** Christian worship with the practices of another religion you are studying. Create a table which explains the similarities and differences between them.

 SUMMARY

- Worship is important because it helps believers express love for God.
- It can be liturgical, non-liturgical, or individual.
- There is a great amount of variety in worship both between and within denominations.

 EXAM-STYLE QUESTIONS

a Outline **three** ways a Christian can worship. (3)

b Describe **two** differences between Christian worship and that of another religion you have studied. (4)

3.2 The Sacraments

What are sacraments?

The **sacraments** are particularly important and significant Christian ceremonies. Many Christians think of the sacraments as signs of God's love – a special holy action that shows a religious truth. For some Christians, for example Catholics, sacraments are more than just signs – they are 'effective signs', which means that they bring about the thing that they symbolise. For instance, **baptism** is not just a sign of the forgiveness of sins, it actually brings about the forgiveness of sins.

For something to be a sacrament, it has to be officially recognised by the Church as having been established by Jesus. Churches differ on this matter. Therefore, some ceremonies, like marriage, might be carried out in all churches, but might not be considered to be an official 'Sacrament' in all churches.

The sacraments recognised by different groups

Various denominations within the Church have different views on the sacraments. The biggest denominations are the Catholic, Orthodox and Protestant Churches. In turn, Protestants are divided into groups, such as Anglicans (including the Church of England) and Non-Conformists (e.g. Quakers, Methodists, Salvation Army and Baptists).

The Catholic council of Trent (1545–1563) agreed that there were seven sacraments (see image A). The Orthodox Church also recognises seven sacraments. In contrast, the Church of England met in 1562 to agree the **39 Articles of Religion**, and Article 25 stated that the Church of England would only recognise two sacraments – baptism and the **eucharist**. In some Protestant churches, for example the Salvation Army and Quakers, no sacraments are officially recognised.

SPECIFICATION FOCUS

The role of the sacraments in Christian life and their practice in two denominations: the role of the sacraments/ordinance as a whole; the nature and importance of the meaning and celebration of baptism and the eucharist in at least two denominations including reference to the 39 Articles XXV–XXXVI; divergent Christian attitudes towards the use and number of sacraments in Orthodox, Catholic and Protestant traditions.

USEFUL TERMS

39 Articles of Religion: A historical record of beliefs (or 'doctrines') held by the Church of England

Anoint: apply oil to a person's head as a sign of holiness and God's approval

Sacrament: an important Christian ceremony

A The seven sacraments of the Catholic Church

Sacraments of initiation			Sacraments of service		Sacraments of healing	
Baptism	Confirmation	Eucharist (mass or holy communion)	Marriage	Taking holy orders	Reconciliation (confession)	**Anointing** the sick with oil

The 39 Articles of Religion

In the mid-16th century, the Church of England had recently split from the Catholic Church, and was feeling the influence of various Protestant denominations. Therefore, in 1562, the Bishops and Archbishops of England came together to discuss matters of belief. Their eventual agreed beliefs would be published under the heading of the 39 Articles. The Articles cover heaven, hell, baptism, creeds, and much more, but the Articles also make some strong statements against various areas of Catholic belief. From that point onwards, priests of the Church of England would need to agree to the 39 Articles before they could be ordained.

Celebrating the sacraments

The sacraments have two important aspects:

- **Physical side:** this can be felt, touched, seen, smelled or tasted, as, for example, the bread and wine in the eucharist.
- **Spiritual side:** each sacrament brings a spiritual blessing to the person involved.

Each sacrament has its own special ceremony, which includes some or all of the following features: saying prayers, singing hymns, making vows, or promises, listening to Bible readings, listening to a sermon.

Baptism

Baptism is the ceremony in which a person formally becomes a member of the Church. It was commanded by Jesus in *Matthew 28: 19*.

The Catholic, Orthodox and Anglican Churches all celebrate baptism of infants (babies and young children). The Quakers and Salvation Army do not have formal baptism at all. The Baptist Church baptises people it considers old enough to decide for themselves that they want to be baptised.

In an infant baptism, a priest pours water three times on the child's head to show that the Trinity has come into their life and that their sins have been washed away. The child's parents and godparents publicly declare their beliefs, and hold a lighted candle to symbolise that they and the child have passed from the darkness of sin into the light of Jesus. In the Catholic Church, the candle is lit from the Paschal candle as a sign of faith in the resurrection of Jesus. The child is then welcomed as a member of the Church.

Some denominations, for example Baptist and Pentecostal Churches, do not celebrate infant baptism, and instead baptise people when they are adults. This is because they believe baptism is a choice that should be made as an adult. They do celebrate the birth of infants, however, and usually will have a 'dedication' service in which the parents and the Church community promise to bring up the child according to Christian values.

Confirmation

When a person freely chooses to conclude the process of baptism, as already begun during their baptism as an infant, they are 'confirmed', usually after attending a course of Bible study. Anglicans usually have to be at least

> ❝There are two Sacraments ordained of Christ our Lord in the Gospel, that is to say, Baptism, and the Supper of the Lord.❞ Those five commonly called Sacraments, that is to say, Confirmation, Penance, Orders, Matrimony, and extreme Unction, are not to be counted for Sacraments of the Gospel...❞
> *(From Article XXV of the 39 Articles of Religion)*

USEFUL TERMS

Baptism: the Christian ceremony that welcomes a person into the Christian community

Eucharist: the ceremony commemorating the Last Supper, involving bread and wine; also called Holy Communion or Mass

> ❝Therefore go and make disciples of all nations, **baptising them** in the name of the Father and of the Son and of the Holy Spirit...❞
> *(Matthew 28: 19)*

What symbolism can you see in this photo? Can you find out its significance? STRETCH

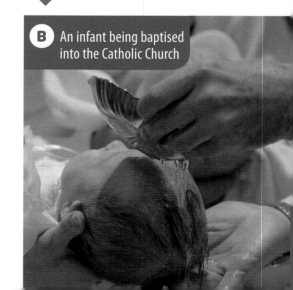

B An infant being baptised into the Catholic Church

12 years old to be confirmed, Catholics have to be at least 8 years old. There is no confirmation service in the Orthodox Church, and instead of Confirmation, Orthodox Christians have the Sacrament of Chrismation, which immediately follows baptism, and involves being anointed with holy oil called Chrism.

The confirmation service is held by the local bishop. Those being confirmed make the same statements of belief as the parents in an infant baptism. The bishop lays hands on the person's head as a sign that the Holy Spirit has entered into the person's life. (In the Catholic Church, the laying on of hands is what actually brings about the gift of the Spirit). The person is then welcomed as a full member of the Church.

Eucharist

The eucharist is accepted by most Christians as a re-enactment of the final meal that Jesus shared with his disciples. At that meal, he spoke of bread and wine as being his body and blood.

The eucharist is called Mass in the Catholic Church, Holy Communion in the Anglican Church and the Lord's supper by the Methodists. It is not celebrated by the Salvation Army.

In Catholic and Anglican Churches today, the priest prays for God's special blessing on bread and wine, which makes them holy. They are then given by the priest to each person taking part in the eucharist. Only those who are baptised or confirmed may take part. They each take a small piece of bread or a wafer and a sip from a single cup (chalice) of wine. In the Orthodox Church, Christians receive bread soaked in wine.

Not all Christians see the eucharist in the same way:

- Catholic and Orthodox Christians believe that the bread and wine change to become the actual body and blood of Jesus. In the Catholic Church this change happens when the bread and wine are blessed and is called transubstantiation. In the Orthodox Church, how or when the bread and wine change is believed to be a mystery.
- Other Christians, including Anglicans, believe that the bread and wine are simply symbolic of Jesus' body and blood to help believers remember his death.
- Catholics believe they should receive the bread and wine at least once a week and some receive it every day.
- Protestants may take the bread and wine less often, perhaps once every few weeks. Some do not receive it at all, for example members of the Salvation Army.

Marriage

The Sacrament of marriage reflects God's everlasting love. It is the legal union of a man and a woman, who promise before God that they will love, honour, cherish and respect each other through sickness, health, through good times and bad times, until they are parted by death.

Taking holy orders

In the Catholic and Orthodox Churches, the Sacrament of holy orders means becoming a deacon, priest, or bishop.

'And he took bread, gave thanks and broke it, and gave it to them, saying, "This is my body given for you; do this in remembrance of me." In the same way, after the supper he took the cup, saying, "This cup is the new covenant in my blood, which is poured out for you.'
(Luke 22: 19–20)

SUPPORT

The **covenant** is an agreement between God and humans, which says that because Jesus died to save people from sin, those who believe in him will have everlasting life in heaven with God.

C The eucharist involves bread and wine

Catholics believe that priests are descended from Jesus' original apostles 2,000 years ago. As a result, priests receive the grace and power of the Holy Spirit and have the privileged ability to administer all of the sacraments apart from the Sacrament of holy orders. Deacons can administer the sacraments of baptism and marriage, and both priests and deacons can preach.

Like Catholic priests, bishops in the Orthodox Church are believed to be the direct successors of the original apostles. Orthodox bishops are required to remain celibate, but priests may be married before they are ordained.

Reconciliation

The Sacrament of Reconciliation (also called Confession) is when a person asks forgiveness for the wrongs they have done. For reconciliation to be effective, the person must be genuinely sorry, have spent time preparing their confession, and be ready to receive God's blessing and forgiveness. In return, they know they have done what they could to right the wrong.

Catholic and Orthodox Christians confess their sins to a priest, who, as God's representative on earth, will then give them God's forgiveness. This may involve the person having to 'do penance', such as saying a particular prayer a set number of times, or carrying out positive actions to right the wrongs caused by their sins.

Anointing the sick

The Sacrament of anointing the sick is based on teaching in the Bible:

> ❝ Is anyone among you ill? Let them call the elders of the church to pray over them and anoint them with oil in the name of the Lord. ❞
> *(James 5: 14)*

In the anointing ceremony, the sick person confesses their sins and prays with the priest. They pray that God will heal them or, if they are dying, that God will forgive their sins and grant them everlasting life in heaven. The priest lays hands on the person to enable God's love to work within them and some olive oil is gently rubbed onto their forehead.

D Anointing the sick

 EXAM-STYLE QUESTIONS

a Outline **three** Christian sacraments. (3)
b Explain **two** reasons why sacraments are important to Christians. (4)

SUMMARY

- The sacraments are significant Christian ceremonies which have been recognised by the Church.
- The Catholic and Orthodox Churches recognise seven sacraments, the Church of England recognise two (baptism and the eucharist), and some churches do not officially recognise any.

BUILD YOUR SKILLS

1 Copy and complete the following table for the main ideas about the sacraments in this unit.

Sacrament	What is involved?	Which Christians recognise it and why?

2 Explain two different approaches to baptism within Christianity.

3 Can the bread and wine really be the body and blood of Jesus? Explain your ideas, referring to different Christian views.

3.3 Prayer

What is prayer?

Prayer is a way of communicating with God, usually through words, and having a personal relationship with him. Prayer may offer praise or thanks to God or ask him for forgiveness or other specific things, for example good health. Christians can pray in many different ways – using set or informal prayers, in public or in private, every day or on special occasions.

Set prayers

Most prayers in an Anglican or Catholic church service are set and formal. They are usually read or sung from a text, such as the *Book of Common Prayer*, and follow a set pattern very familiar to believers. The most famous formal prayer is 'The Lord's Prayer' (see figure **A**), which Jesus taught to his followers. It is a special prayer because it covers the needs of all believers.

Informal prayer

Some prayer is much more informal. This type of prayer features in Evangelical and Charismatic churches, where prayers are not often written down. Instead, prayer tends to be much more spontaneous, because believers say that they are led by the Holy Spirit to choose words to express how they feel at the time.

SPECIFICATION FOCUS

The nature and purpose of prayer: the nature of and examples of the different types of prayer; set prayers; informal prayer and the Lord's Prayer including Matthew 6: 5–14; when each type might be used and why; divergent Christian attitudes towards the importance of each type of prayer for Christians today.

USEFUL TERMS

Prayer: a way of communicating with God

A What does 'The Lord's Prayer' mean?

'Our Father in heaven, — This is a personal and loving response to God.

hallowed be your name, — Your name is holy and special.

your kingdom come, — May God's kingdom come to our world.

your will be done, — May God's will be carried out.

on earth as it is in heaven. — May God be in charge.

Give us today our daily bread. — Give us all we need to survive.

And forgive us our debts, — Forgive the wrongs we have done.

as we also have forgiven our debtors. — Help us to forgive those who have wronged us.

And lead us not into temptation, — Keep us from being tempted to do wrong.

but deliver us from the evil one.' — Keep us from doing evil.

(Matthew 6: 9–13)

Private prayer

Believers can also pray in private settings, such as their own homes. They might say their prayers aloud or offer them silently to God.

> ‘When you pray, go into your room, close the door and pray to your father, who is unseen. Then your Father, who sees what is done in secret, will reward you.’
> *(Matthew 6: 6)*

Special purposes of prayer

Christians use different prayers, depending on what they want to say to God. These can be grouped into different types:

Thanksgiving: to thank God for all that they have.
Contrition: to tell God what they have done wrong and ask for forgiveness.
Supplication: to ask God for something for themselves or others.
Intercession: to ask God to help other people.
Worship: to give honour and respect to God.

Divergent Christian attitudes

Most Christians will use both set and informal prayer to communicate with God. The Lord's Prayer is used regularly in most denominations, as Christians like to follow the example set by Jesus. Christians who prefer to pray more using set prayers find comfort in using words that have been said throughout history and have also been authorised by their Church. Reciting these aloud as a community also increases a sense of shared belief and unity. Christians who prefer praying informally might particularly appreciate the personal nature of communicating how they are feeling with God. These Christians also value praying aloud in groups, and those with them will often say 'Amen' after an individual has prayed to show that they agree with the prayer.

B Many Christians feel better by being able to talk directly and privately to God

C 'Praying hands', a drawing by Albrecht Dürer (c. 1508ᴄᴇ)

BUILD YOUR SKILLS

1   Read the Lord's Prayer on page 85. What different things do Christians ask for or say in this prayer?   **SUPPORT**

2   Why do Christians pray? Write a short paragraph to explain.

3   If God knows everything, what is the point of praying? What would a Christian argue?   **STRETCH**

SUMMARY

- Prayers can be set, informal or private.
- There are prayers for different purposes, and believers differ in their views on the importance of certain types of prayer.

EXAM-STYLE QUESTIONS

b   Explain **two** reasons why prayer is important to Christians. (4)

d   'Prayer should be informal.' Evaluate this statement considering arguments for and against. In your response you should:
- refer to Christian teachings
- refer to different Christian points of view
- reach a justified conclusion. (15)

3.4 Pilgrimage

What is pilgrimage?

A **pilgrimage** is a special journey to a place of religious significance. It is undertaken by a pilgrim, who is making the journey in order to increase their religious faith. It may be a long journey to another country or a shorter one to a sacred place nearer to home.

The first Christian pilgrimages date from the fourth century, when travellers visited the Holy Land (now called Israel) to see places linked to the life of Jesus. Early pilgrims also visited Rome, other sites linked to the Apostles and the saints, and places where **visions** of the Virgin Mary were said to have occurred.

Today, pilgrimage is still popular, with Christians making journeys to Rome, the Holy Land and **shrines** all around the world. A pilgrimage should have a real impact on the pilgrim and involves some or all of the following aspects: feeling closer to God, discovering special rituals, objects and places, having religious and spiritual experiences, praying and meditating, seeking a cure for sickness.

Divergent Christian views on pilgrimage

The Catholic Church teaches about the importance of pilgrimage in the Christian life:

> ❝Pilgrimages evoke our earthly journey toward heaven and are traditionally very special occasions for renewal in prayer. ❞
> *Catechism of the Catholic Church, 2691*

In other words, pilgrimages are believed to be a special opportunity to pray and experience closeness to God. In many Protestant churches, pilgrimage is equally important, although the sites of significance may sometimes be different (for example, Christians who do not recognise the authority of the Pope, as Catholics do, may not view a pilgrimage to Rome in the same way).

Some Protestant churches do not place as much emphasis on pilgrimage. Whilst journeying and praying for the sake of God is something they might encourage, pilgrimage is not considered to be a central part of Christian life.

SPECIFICATION FOCUS

Pilgrimage: the nature, history and purpose of pilgrimage, including interpretations of Luke 2: 41–43; the significance of the places people go on pilgrimage; divergent Christian teachings about whether pilgrimage is important for Christians today, with specific reference to Catholic and Protestant understandings; the activities associated with, and significance of, Jerusalem, Iona, Taizé and Walsingham.

What do you think believers gain from pilgrimage? Is it just a religious holiday?

SUPPORT

The Canterbury Tales, written by Geoffrey Chaucer around 1390 CE, is a collection of stories told by pilgrims on a pilgrimage from London to Canterbury Cathedral.

STRETCH

A A medieval pilgrimage

The pilgrimage to Jerusalem

The most famous place of Christian pilgrimage is Jerusalem in Israel (the Holy Land). It is where most of Jesus' ministry took place, so pilgrims feel it is important to go to different sites in the city to think about the events that took place there.

In the Gospel of Luke, Jesus himself made a pilgrimage with his parents to Jerusalem, at the age of twelve. When it was time to leave, his parents could not find Jesus. When they finally found him, he was in the temple, sitting and listening to teachers, and he said: "Why were you searching for me? […] "Didn't you know I had to be in my Father's house?" (*Luke 2: 49*). Modern pilgrims aim to follow Jesus' example and look for opportunities to be close to God. Pilgrims today visit:

B Modern pilgrims on the Via Dolorosa, the road believed to have been taken by Jesus on his way to be crucified

- The Mount of Olives, where Jesus often taught his followers
- The room of the Last Supper
- The Garden of Gethsemane, where Jesus was arrested
- The Western Wall, remains of the Temple
- The tomb of the Virgin Mary
- The Church of the Holy Sepulchre, where Jesus was crucified and buried

The pilgrimage to Iona

Iona Abbey, on the island of Iona, off the west coast of Scotland, is one of the UK's oldest sites of pilgrimage. It was founded by St Columba in 563 CE and became the focal point for the spread of Christianity throughout Scotland. The abbey was extensively restored in 1899 and in 1938, when the Iona Community was founded. This Christian community is based on worship, peace and social justice, and welcomes all believers to share in this ministry today.

The pilgrimage to Taizé

Another important place for Christian pilgrimage today is a monastic order in the small village of Taizé in central France. The Taizé Community was founded by Roger Schütz, known as Brother Roger, in 1940. Today, it has over 100 members, and thousands of pilgrims visit to share the community's way of life.

The community prays together three times a day and is devoted to peace and justice through prayer and meditation. It seeks to unite people of all races and encourages pilgrims to live in the spirit of kindness, simplicity and reconciliation. Importance is also placed on music, including songs and chants in many languages.

SUPPORT

People who live **monastic** lives, such as **monks** and **nuns**, have chosen to dedicate their lives to prayer and worship, usually whilst living in a **monastery** with others.

The pilgrimage to Walsingham

A popular English site for Christian pilgrimage is the Shrine of Our Lady of Walsingham in Norfolk.

It is said to be the place where Lady Richeldis de Faverches saw a vision of the Virgin Mary in 1061 CE. According to tradition, the Virgin showed Lady Richeldis a vision of the house where the Angel Gabriel told Mary that she would be the mother of Jesus. Lady Richeldis built a copy of the house on the spot where she had the vision. Known as the Holy House, it became a place of pilgrimage.

In the centuries that followed, thousands of pilgrims went to Walsingham, including Henry VIII and Queen Catherine of Aragon. Later in Henry's reign, the shrine was destroyed.

After restoration, Walsingham was re-opened to regular pilgrimage in the 1920s. In 1938 it was enlarged to form the area known today, including a Catholic shrine, an Anglican shrine and the Orthodox Church of St Seraphim. There are often, therefore, pilgrimages of mixed denominations to Walsingham.

> **USEFUL TERMS**
>
> **Pilgrimage:** a journey to a religious or holy place
>
> **Shrine:** a holy place
>
> **Vision:** seeing or hearing someone or something holy

 BUILD YOUR SKILLS

1 Copy and complete the following table for important pilgrimage sites.

Site of pilgrimage	What does it represent?	Why is it important for Christians?
Jerusalem		
Iona		
Taizé		
Walsingham		

2 a Which of the following statements, if any, do you agree with? Explain why.
- 'Some sites of pilgrimage are more convincing than others.'
- 'Pilgrims are just wishful thinkers.'
- 'Pilgrimage is still important in today's world.'
- 'On pilgrimage, the journey is as important as the destination.'

   b With a partner, discuss whether pilgrimages are worthwhile or a waste of time.

3 Many thousands of young people visit Taizé each year (see image **C**). Do you think they have to be Christians to benefit from the visit? Why/why not?

C Worship at Taizé

 SUMMARY

- Pilgrimage has a very long history and is still important today.
- Jerusalem, Iona, Taizé and Walsingham are important pilgrimage sites.
- Pilgrimage helps believers to understand more about God and their faith.
- It can give believers a strong religious or spiritual experience.

> **? EXAM-STYLE QUESTIONS**
>
> a Outline **three** reasons why pilgrimage is important to Christians. (3)
>
> d 'Every Christian should go on a pilgrimage.'
> Evaluate this statement considering arguments for and against. In your response you should:
> - refer to Christian teachings
> - refer to different Christian points of view
> - reach a justified conclusion. (15)

Christians use celebrations to remember and give thanks for the most important events in their faith. Celebrations take different forms to reflect the nature of the event. Some, like Christmas and Easter Sunday, are times of great rejoicing. Others, such as Good Friday, are times for quiet reflection.

Christmas

There are two accounts of the birth of Jesus, given in the Gospels of Luke and Matthew. According to Luke's Gospel, God sent the Angel Gabriel to tell a woman called Mary, who was a virgin, that she would be the mother of God's son. She accepted God's will and became pregnant. She and her husband Joseph travelled to the town of Bethlehem. There, she gave birth to Jesus and was visited by shepherds. The Gospel of Matthew includes an account of the visit of the wise men, or 'Magi', from the east.

The whole season of Christmastide runs for 12 nights after 25 December to 6 January, which is when Jesus was shown to the wise men. The 6 January is therefore called **Epiphany** or Twelfth Night.

As a festival, Christmas shares much in common with other festivals at that time.

- It is just after mid-winter, when the sun begins to shine more and the days start to grow longer.
- It is near the Winter Solstice, when mistletoe was seen as a sign of God's blessing.
- Holly, also a Christian symbol, was used by ancient people as a protection from evil.

In medieval times, Christmas was a time for feasting and fun. However, in the seventeenth century, people were not allowed to have celebrations because they were believed by Puritans to be excessive and a distraction from core Christian beliefs. In 1644 Christmas was banned altogether. Christmas became popular again in the nineteenth century when cards, decorations and Christmas trees were introduced.

Today, Christian churches hold special services, including carol services and a **vigil** before Christmas, midnight mass on Christmas Eve, and a special service of celebration on Christmas morning, which may include a **nativity** play.

SPECIFICATION FOCUS

Christian religious celebrations: the nature and history of Christian festivals in the church year, including Christmas and Easter; the significance of celebrating Advent and Christmas; the significance of celebrating Holy Week and Easter with reference to interpretations of 1 Corinthians 15: 12–34.

USEFUL TERMS

Advent: a coming

Epiphany: a moment of suddenly revealing something surprising or great

Holy week: the week before Easter

Nativity: the birth of someone

Prophecy: a message from God in which he communicates his will

Vigil: staying awake at night in order to pray; also the name given to the celebration of a festival on the eve before the festival itself

A Children's nativity plays are an important part of Church life

B Candlelight vigil

Advent

Advent starts on the Sunday nearest 30 November. It marks the start of the Christian year and is a time of preparation for Christmas. On the first Sunday of Advent, Christians light one of the four candles on Advent wreaths. On each of the next three Sundays before Christmas, they light one more candle. This is to remember the 'light' of Jesus that is about to come into the world.

Holy week

Holy week is the week just before Easter, beginning with Palm Sunday and ending with Holy Saturday. It is the final week of Lent, the six-week period of self-examination when most Christians pray, say sorry and try to make amends for their wrongdoings, fast and give to the poor in preparation for celebrating Jesus' resurrection on Easter Sunday. Holy week is also a time of solemn church services, as Christians remember the final days and death of Jesus. The following events are remembered during the week:

- **Palm Sunday:** Jesus' arrival in Jerusalem on a donkey, when huge crowds greeted him and threw down palm leaves. This fulfilled an ancient prophecy that the Messiah would arrive in this way. Today, Christians receive small palm crosses to remind them of the prophecy and the death of Jesus.

- **Holy Monday:** Mary anointing Jesus with oil at Bethany as a sign of God's approval *(John 12:3)*.

- **Holy Tuesday:** Jesus predicting that Judas would betray him and Peter would deny that he knew Jesus.

- **Holy Wednesday:** Judas arranging with the high priests to betray Jesus.

- **Maundy Thursday:** Jesus washing the disciples' feet and the Last Supper. The washing of feet was a symbolic act to show that the disciples must be humble and serve others ('Maundy' means 'commandment'). On this day, churches may hold a meal reflecting the original Last Supper.

- **Good Friday:** Jesus' death on the cross. For Christians, this is a solemn day of processions or re-enacting the events leading up to the crucifixion.

- **Holy Saturday:** Jesus going to hell and preaching to the dead. In the evening, many Christians hold a vigil. For example, on the eve of Holy Saturday, Catholic Christians have an Easter vigil at which they celebrate the resurrection of Jesus. This is the most solemn liturgy that the Catholic Church celebrates.

'Shout, daughter of Jerusalem! See your king comes to you, righteous and having salvation, gentle and riding on a donkey.' *(Zechariah 9: 9)*

'I tell you the truth, one of you is going to betray me.' *(John 13: 20)*

'A new command I give you: Love one another.' *(John 13: 34)*

Easter Sunday

Easter Sunday celebrates the resurrection of Jesus from the dead. Jesus had been buried in a cave tomb with an enormous stone rolled across the entrance. On Sunday morning, Mary Magdalene, then others of Jesus' followers, found that the stone had been rolled away and the tomb was empty. Soon after, they saw Jesus – he had risen from the dead.

In 1 Corinthians 15, Paul writes to the Corinthian church about the resurrection. Members of the church at the time were in disagreement about whether the dead could be raised. Paul emphasises the fundamental importance of the resurrection to Christianity:

> ❝For what I received I passed on to you as of first importance: that Christ died for our sins according to the Scriptures, that he was buried, that he was raised on the third day...❞
> *(1 Corinthians 15: 3–4)*

 c The empty tomb; which people can you see represented here?

He writes, 'by this gospel you are saved' (1 Corinthians 15: 2), in other words Christians have access to eternal life because of the resurrection of Jesus.

> ❝And if Christ has not been raised, our preaching is useless and so is your faith.❞
> *(1 Corinthians 15: 14)*

Read the rest of Paul's argument in 1 Corinthians 15: 12–34. What are his key points? **STRETCH**

Most Christians today believe in the physical resurrection of Jesus, but some more liberal Christians believe that the resurrection should be interpreted metaphorically. Mainstream and liberal Christians alike celebrate this story on Easter Sunday, worshiping and praising Jesus in church services.

 BUILD YOUR SKILLS

1 Explain the significance of each of the following: Christmas, Advent, Holy week, Easter.

2 Which of the following statements, if any, do you agree with? Explain why.
   - 'Easter is about the death of Jesus, not about Easter eggs.'
   - 'The most important Christian celebration day is Easter Sunday.'
   - 'Religious celebrations have no importance in today's world.'

3 According to Paul, why is the resurrection of Jesus so important?

 SUMMARY

- Christian celebrations include Advent, Christmas, Holy week and Easter.
- These celebrations help believers to remember the importance of events in Jesus' life.
- They also help believers to feel closer to God and understand more about their faith.

? **EXAM-STYLE QUESTIONS**

a Outline **three** features of Christmas for Christians. (3)

d 'Easter is the most important Christian festival.'
   Evaluate this statement considering arguments for and against. In your response you should:
   - refer to Christian teachings
   - refer to different Christian points of view
   - reach a justified conclusion. (15)

3.6 The future of the Church

Growth of the Christian Church

Christianity has more followers than any other religion and **Pentecostalism** is one of the fastest growing denominations. There are 2.4 billion Christians in the world today and the number is growing. The biggest increases recently have been in Africa, where there are 541 million Christians, with 33,000 people joining the faith every day. The Church is also growing in Asia and the Middle East, especially in Nepal, China and Saudi Arabia.

Much of this growth is due to the work of **missionaries**, who preach from the Bible and invite people to **convert** to the Christian faith. However, people in many countries are also actively turning away from traditional beliefs to join faiths that seem to offer more – enthusiasm, lively worship and a promise of eternal life.

Christianity in the UK

In contrast, the Christian Church in the UK and Western Europe is going through a difficult time. A recent survey noted that although 64% of UK residents say they are Christian, the number of local churchgoers is falling quite rapidly. Many churches closed between 2010 and 2016 – 168 Anglican, 500 Methodist and 100 Catholic.

However, the numbers of people joining Pentecostal and Evangelical churches has been steadily increasing. Between 2010 and 2016, 600 Pentecostal churches opened. This growth seems to be driven in part by people coming to live in the UK, particularly from Africa, the Caribbean and South America, but these churches have also seen a steady increase in UK worshippers.

Christian missionary work

The Church has a **mission** to spread the Christian faith. It does this by sending missionaries around the world. As well as preaching to people about Jesus, missionary work may also include working among the poor to build hospitals and schools, nursing, and teaching.

SPECIFICATION FOCUS

The future of the Christian Church: Church growth, the history and purpose of missionary and evangelical work including reference to Mark 16: 9–20 and John 20: 21–22; divergent ways this is put into practice by Church locally, nationally and globally; Christian attitudes to why evangelical work is important for the Church and for individual Christians.

USEFUL TERMS

Convert: to change from one set of beliefs to another

Mission: sending individuals or groups to spread the Christian message

Missionary: a person who preaches and invites people to convert to the Christian faith

Pentecostalism: a Protestant movement that puts special emphasis on a direct and personal relationship with God through the Holy Spirit

A A church community in Rwanda, Africa

The history of missionary work

The first missionaries were the original followers of Jesus, who obeyed his command called the Great Commission. With the help of the Holy Spirit, the followers were commanded to preach the gospel to all of creation:

> ❝He said to them, "**Go into all the world and preach the gospel to all creation**. Whoever believes and is baptized will be saved, but whoever does not believe will be condemned.'❞
> *(Mark 16: 15)*

> ❝Again Jesus said, "Peace be with you! As the Father has sent me, I am sending you." And with that he breathed on them and said, "**Receive the Holy Spirit...**"❞
> *(John 20: 21–22)*

The most famous early missionary was St Paul, whose mission took him as far as Rome – thousands of miles from where he began. In the following centuries, Christian missionaries went to many other parts of the world.

Inviting non-Christians to convert to Christianity

Spreading the teachings of Jesus

Establishing monasteries and churches

Setting up and running schools and colleges

Purposes of missionary work

Setting up and staffing hospitals and medical centres

Providing sanitation and clean water

Translating the Bible into every language

Missionary work today

Many Christians still feel the responsibility to tell others of their faith. Whilst some become missionaries, others show their faith at home in the way they conduct their everyday lives.

Most Christian countries still send missionaries abroad, but they also receive them from elsewhere. Typically, the UK sends out 15,000 missionaries a year, whilst 10,000 others travel into the UK.

However, some people criticise missionary work abroad on the basis that missionaries:

- might only spread Western values
- can infect local populations with foreign germs and diseases
- have caused conflicts and even wars in the past
- could be accused of using natural disasters as an opportunity to 'convert' those who are suffering.

The growth of the Pentecostal Church in Britain is also a type of 'reverse mission', with immigrants drawing people back into churches here.

On a local level, churches are encouraged to be open and welcoming to everyone, not just practising Christians, often holding events to draw non-believers in.

B A school in Cambodia set up by missionaries

Christian evangelistic work

Missionary work involves **evangelism**, preaching the Christian faith in order to invite those of other faiths or none to convert to Christianity. Evangelists are often missionaries, but they might be skilled in preaching to large numbers in their own country.

Evangelists are inspired by biblical teaching to speak clearly, fearlessly and respectfully, and see themselves as following a call from God.

> ❛Pray also for me… so that I will fearlessly make known the mystery of the gospel…❜
> *(Ephesians 6: 19)*

> **SUPPORT**
>
> The word **evangelism** comes from the Greek word euaggellion, which means gospel or good news.

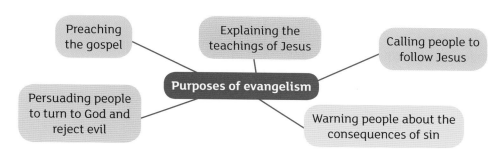

- Preaching the gospel
- Explaining the teachings of Jesus
- Calling people to follow Jesus
- **Purposes of evangelism**
- Persuading people to turn to God and reject evil
- Warning people about the consequences of sin

> 🔑 **USEFUL TERMS**
>
> **Alpha:** a course run by churches and local Christian groups which enables people to find out more about the Christian faith in a relaxed setting
>
> **Evangelism:** preaching the gospel in order to attract new believers

Evangelism today

Modern evangelists can be very public figures. Some use television, radio, the Internet, social media, drama, music or comedy to communicate their message. A few appear on television's 'God Channel'. Others speak to huge crowds at Christian events.

However, for many Christians today, evangelism is something that happens naturally in conversation and discussion, as they talk about their faith with others.

 CASE STUDY: ALPHA

One organised way that churches enable evangelism in a relaxed format is through **Alpha**, which was started in an Anglican church in 1977. At first, it aimed to help church members understand the basics of the Christian faith. It soon began to be used as an introduction for anyone interested in learning about Christianity.

It now offers 'an opportunity to explore the meaning of life' through a series of talks and discussions in all sorts of places from homes to offices, churches to prisons. The idea has now been adopted by other denominations worldwide and has generated related courses such as relationship courses.

C A group of young people taking part in Alpha

> **STRETCH**
>
> Find out more about Alpha by visiting **uk.alpha.org**. What happens on a typical course? What questions do people discuss?

The importance of evangelistic work

This work is important for the Church as a whole and for individual Christians. It:

- enables Christians to obey the 'Great Commission' of Jesus
- encourages Christians to tell other people about their faith
- can help the poor and suffering to have hope
- can occur alongside improvements to education and healthcare
- keeps the Christian message alive and relevant to life today
- brings many new Christians to the Church.

BUILD YOUR SKILLS

1   Copy and complete the following table for Christian missionary and evangelical work.

	What does it mean?	Examples	Why is it important for Christians?
Christian mission			
Evangelism			

2   a   Imagine a conversation about evangelism between three teenagers – one is an evangelical Christian, one is a member of another faith, and the third is an atheist. Write a short conversation between them in which:
- each says why their view is right
- each tries to prove that the others are wrong.

   b   Which teenager do you think offers the best answers? Why?

3   a   With a partner or in a group, discuss the advantages and disadvantages of:
- evangelising on television
- taking part in the Alpha Course.

   b   Write down your conclusions.

SUMMARY

- Christian Church membership is growing globally, but is falling in the UK.
- Missionary and evangelical work preach the Christian faith and invite people to convert to Christianity.
- Missionaries also help the needy.

EXAM-STYLE QUESTIONS

a   Outline **three** purposes of Christian missionary work. (3)

c   Explain **two** reasons why evangelism is important to Christians. In your answer you must refer to a source of wisdom and authority. (5)

SPECIFICATION FOCUS

The role and importance of the local church in the local community: how and why it helps the individual believer and the local area; local parish activities including interpretations of 1 Peter 5: 1–4, ecumenism, outreach work, the centre of Christian identity and worship through living practices.

The importance of the local church to the parish

Most Christians belong to a **parish** – a community of local believers within a particular denomination. The care of the parish and its people is entrusted to a parish priest. The local church building plays an important role in the community's life together. Living in that community encourages individual Christians to put their faith into action in everyday living practices, such as being a good neighbour and caring for those in need.

A place for Christians to gather as a community

A place to learn about Christian beliefs and way of life

A regular pattern of worship through church services

Special services for baptisms, weddings and funerals

Care and advice from the priest and other church officials

A The parish church is the centre of local religious life

How the local church helps individual believers and the local area

The Bible calls the Church 'the body of Christ' and Christians believe that the Church is holy and belongs to God. The Church's mission is to preach the gospel and to make God's kingdom a reality in their own local community.

Each **local church** follows that mission. It also supports believers in following Jesus' teachings in their own lives, encouraging them to be good people. Local churches carry out their mission in various ways, by:

- offering the church as a community centre to bring local people together
- giving spiritual support to the sick
- praying for those in need
- supporting groups that campaign for justice and peace
- offering moral guidance
- telling others about Jesus (evangelism)
- **outreach** to children, the poor and the needy
- supporting young adults with advice on jobs, training, finance and finding a home
- giving friendship and help to the elderly
- raising money for charity.

B Is it really the role of local churches to feed the poor?

Should local churches be used just by believers or also by non-believers? **STRETCH**

Ecumenism

There is a movement within the Church that tries to create unity and friendship between different Christian denominations. It is called **ecumenism**. Supporters say that closer union will lead to:

- tolerance of different ideas
- mutual understanding of the Christian faith
- less discrimination and conflict
- friendship among Christians.

C Pope Francis meets Archbishop Justin Welby and his wife at the Vatican in 2013

BUILD YOUR SKILLS

1   What do these terms mean, and why are they important? Parish, the local church, ecumenism.

2   **a**   What are Christians being taught to do in these Bible verses?

> ❛To the elders among you [...] Be shepherds of God's flock that is under your care, watching over them – not because you must, but because you are willing, as God wants you to be; not pursuing dishonest gain, but eager to serve; not lording it over those entrusted to you, but being examples to the flock. And when the Chief Shepherd appears, you will receive the crown of glory that will never fade away.❜
> *(1 Peter 5: 1–4)*

> ❛Always be prepared to give an answer to everyone who asks you to give the reason for the hope that you have.❜
> *(1 Peter 3: 15)*

> ❛Whoever welcomes one of these little children in my name welcomes me.❜
> *(Mark 9: 37)*

   b   How might a Christian put each of these teachings into living practice today?

USEFUL TERMS

Ecumenism: a movement that tries to bring different Christian denominations closer together

Local church: a meeting place for local believers and the community of believers who gather there

Outreach: an activity to provide services to people in need

Parish: a community of local believers within a particular denomination

SUMMARY

- Parish churches are the centre of local religious life but also welcome atheists.
- They preach the Christian faith and help the needy.
- They offer advice and special services for the important events in people's lives.
- The different denominations of the Christian Church are working together through ecumenism to create greater understanding with each other.

EXAM-STYLE QUESTIONS

a   Outline **three** ways that the local church serves its local community. (3)

b   Explain **two** reasons why ecumenism is important to Christians. (4)

3.8 The worldwide Church

What is the role of the Church in the worldwide community?

The Church exists in every nation and aims to have a positive spiritual impact on the world. Its roles include:

- representing Jesus on earth
- bringing the gospel to all people
- helping the poor, the sick and the needy
- promoting friendships
- bringing together as a community all the people who want to know and love God.

The Church is important within the global community because it encourages peace and harmony between individuals and countries, and teaches and tries to set a good example of living a moral life. It also organises charity work, supports the work of its missionaries and helps Christians in need around the world.

The Church also has powerful influence in debates on:

- Abortion
- Injustice
- Marriage
- Moral issues
- Political decisions
- Poverty
- Same-sex relationships.

SPECIFICATION FOCUS

The role and importance of the Church in the worldwide community: how and why it works for reconciliation and the problems faced by the persecuted Church; divergent Christian responses to teachings about charity, including 1 Corinthians 13 and Matthew 25: 31–46; the work of Christian Aid, what they do and why.

'Wherever we see the Word of God purely preached and heard, there a church of God exists.'
Theologian John Calvin (1509–1564)

A The world listens to South Africa's Archbishop Desmond Tutu, who was awarded the 1984 Nobel Peace Prize for his key role in fighting against racial discrimination in his homeland

What is reconciliation?

Reconciliation mends broken relationships, bringing peace and harmony between individuals, groups or countries. Today, the Church seeks to reconcile relationships around the world because Jesus taught, 'As I have loved you, so you must love one another' *(John 13: 34)* and because the Bible says:

> ❝ All this is from God, who reconciled us to himself through Christ and gave us the ministry of reconciliation. ❞
> *(2 Corinthians 5: 18)*

The Church brings together people of different, and often opposing, beliefs to help them reach a reconciliation. It offers prayer, friendship and advice, as well as financial help and expert practical help in difficult situations. Two examples are the Ecumenical Movement and the World Council of Churches.

> **SUPPORT**
> Have you ever fallen out with someone? Did you make up? What steps were needed in order to 'reconcile' with them?

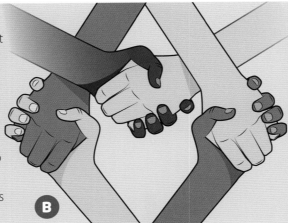

Ecumenical Movement

Aims to bring Christians of different and opposing viewpoints together by:

- praying and seeking guidance
- arranging meetings to share viewpoints and situations
- getting churches and groups to work together
- holding conferences and events around the world.

World Council of Churches

Seeks reconciliation and peace for people around the world by:

- organising days of prayer
- campaigning for peace and human rights
- responding to calls for help and support
- speaking out against oppression and terrorism
- supporting missionaries.

What is persecution?

Persecution is the ill-treatment of an individual or group, usually on the grounds of religion, politics or ethnicity. Another word for it is **oppression**. Globally, persecution happens on a daily basis. Members or groups within various different faiths have experienced persecution, but a minority who claim allegiance with a particular faith can also be persecutors themselves, often where two different belief systems collide. For example, there is a history of violence between Christian and Muslim groups in Nigeria, with atrocities carried out by both sides.

> **STRETCH**
> Do you think that people should always seek reconciliation? Are there some circumstances, such as persecution, where reconciliation seems impossible?

Global persecution of Christians is often referred to as 'the persecuted Church', and takes place in many countries, for instance China, North Korea, and India. According to the International Society for Human Rights, 80% of all religious discrimination in the world is currently directed at Christians. It has also been estimated that 100,000 Christians die every year because of their faith.

Former Chief Rabbi Jonathan Sacks told the House of Lords that the persecution of Christians is *'one of the crimes against humanity of our time'*. However, very few

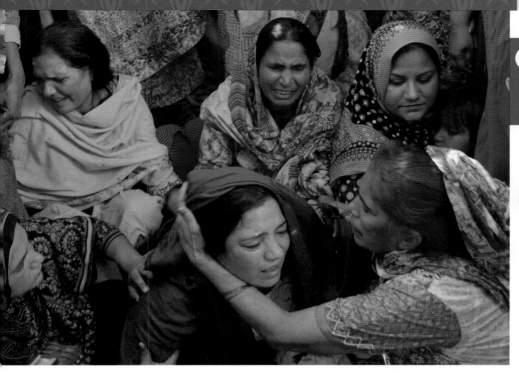

C Pakistani Christians mourn after hundreds of people are killed or injured during Easter celebrations in 2016

people in the wealthy countries of 'the West' know about this persecution. One victim said:

> ❝Does anybody hear our cry? How many atrocities must we endure before somebody comes to our aid?❞

Teachings about charity

Christians have a duty to help those in need. This is called **charity**. The Bible says that followers of Jesus must 'love your neighbour as yourself' *(Mark 12: 31)*, and that everything they own comes from God and that they look after it for him (see stewardship on 1.2).

> ❝Go, sell everything you have and give it to the poor, and you will have treasure in heaven.❞
> *(Mark 10: 21)*

Although this type of giving is central to Christian teaching, many Christians believe it is especially important to do it quietly. This is because Jesus said:

> ❝Be careful not to practise your righteousness in front of others to be seen by them. If you do, you will have no reward from your Father in heaven... [Give your gifts] in secret. Then your Father, who sees what is done in secret, will reward you.❞
> *(Matthew 6: 1, 4)*

D The Salvation Army is an international charitable organisation as well as a Church, whose mission includes 'serving suffering humanity'

St Paul teaches that giving to charity ought to be joyful, and that people should not be forced to give:

> ❝ Each of you should give what you have decided in your heart to give, not reluctantly or under compulsion, for God loves a cheerful giver. ❞
> *(2 Corinthians 9: 7)*

One of Jesus' most powerful teachings on charity is the parable of the sheep and goats *(Matthew 25, 31–46)*. In it he tells believers that, whenever they give to the poor, they are giving to him:

> ❝ ...whatever you did for one of the least of these brothers and sisters of mine, you did for me. ❞
> *(Matthew 25: 40)*

The most important aspect of Christian charity is love:

> ❝ If I give all I possess to the poor... but do not have love, I gain nothing. ❞
> *(1 Corinthians 13: 3)*

Divergent Christian responses

Christians may respond in a variety of ways to these teachings. Some will give charity and tell no one that they have done it, whereas others will discuss it so as to encourage others to give. Often, Christians will ask God to help them to give joyfully, especially because giving involves a degree of sacrifice and it requires love and compassion. Many Christians will give regular financial gifts to the poor, but giving is not always financial: it can also involve time, effort, and skills dedicated to serving people in need.

Christian Aid

One of the ways believers, and non-believers, can help those in need is to donate to charities like Christian Aid. This is the official relief and development agency of 41 Churches. Much of the money donated to it comes from individual Christians and churches, particularly during Christian Aid Week.

Christian Aid works with local organisations around the world where the need is greatest, regardless of religion or race. It is founded on Christian principles of justice and fairness for all and seeks to obey Jesus' teaching to love one another. Its mission statement is:

> ❝ Christian Aid insists the world can and must be swiftly changed to one where everyone can live a full life, free from poverty. ❞

SUPPORT
Christians have a profound love and respect for Jesus, and in this teaching he is telling them to treat others with the same respect that they have for him.

STRETCH
Why is love so important for Christians giving to charity? Isn't the actual gift the most important thing?

E Christian Aid and partners distributing relief material in the Kathmandu Valley following the Nepal earthquake in May 2015

It aims to help the poor to help themselves and often uses the saying,

> 'Give a man a fish, feed him for a day; teach a man to fish, feed him for life.'

Christian Aid operates in three main ways:

- It gives immediate aid such as first aid, food, shelter and clothing in times of disaster. In 2014, it gave emergency help during the famine in South Sudan and the Ebola disease outbreak in Sierra Leone, and in 2015 after the earthquake in Nepal.
- It gives long-term aid and education to help the poor feed themselves. For example, it has provided medical care, clean water and farming equipment in many countries, including Ethiopia, Malawi and Afghanistan.
- It runs political campaigns. In 2012, it organised marches in London against climate change and for more provision for the poor.

Christian Aid also works for reconciliation, defends the poor against the rich and powerful, works to end oppressive debt, and campaigns for justice and human rights.

BUILD YOUR SKILLS

1 Copy and complete the following table for the Church in the worldwide community.

	What does it mean?	**How does it impact the Church?**
Reconciliation		
Persecution		
Charity		

2 'Charity begins at home.' Is it right to give charity and financial aid to overseas countries when there is poverty and need in the UK?
   a How would a Christian answer this and why?
   b What is your own view?

3 Find out more about the work of Christian Aid. Can you link what they say and do to specific Christian teachings? **STRETCH**

SUMMARY

- The Christian Church seeks to have a positive impact on the world.
- It preaches the gospel all around the world.
- It helps the needy and tries to influence debate on many global issues.
- It works for reconciliation.
- Many Christians around the world are persecuted for their faith.
- The Bible teaches that Christians must give charity to those in need and Christian Aid is the official Church charity for carrying out that work.

? EXAM-STYLE QUESTIONS

b Explain **two** ways that Christian Aid works to relieve poverty. (4)
c Explain **two** reasons why giving to charity is important to Christians. In your answer you must refer to a source of wisdom and authority. (5)

Revision

BUILD YOUR SKILLS

Look at the list of 'I can' statements below and think carefully about how confident you are. Use the following code to rate each of the statements. Be honest!

Green – very confident. What is your evidence for this?

Orange – quite confident. What is your target? Be specific.

Red – not confident. What is your target? Be specific.

A self-assessment revision checklist is available on *Kerboodle*

I can...

- Describe the different ways that Christians worship, including liturgical, non-liturgical and individual, and explain when and why each form might be used

- Explain different Christian attitudes towards liturgical and non-liturgical forms of worship including reference to different denominations

- Explain what sacraments are and why they are important

- Describe the meaning and celebration of baptism and the Eucharist in at least two denominations, including reference to a source of wisdom and authority

- Describe different Christian attitudes towards the use and number of sacraments in Orthodox, Catholic and Protestant traditions

- Give examples of different kinds of prayer, with reference to a source of wisdom and authority

- Explain when each type of prayer might be used and why

- Describe different Christian attitudes towards the importance of each type of prayer for Christians today

- Explain what pilgrimage is and why people go on pilgrimages

- Describe the activities associated with different Christian pilgrimages

- Explain different Christian teachings about whether pilgrimage is important for Christians today, with reference to Catholic and Protestant understandings

- Explain the origins and importance of Advent and Christmas

- Explain the origins and importance of Holy Week and Easter, with reference to a source of wisdom and authority

- Explain the meaning of the terms mission and evangelism

- Explain the history and purpose of missionary and evangelistic work in the Church, with reference to a source of wisdom and authority

- Describe some different ways that this work is put into practice by the Church

- Describe Christian attitudes to why evangelistic work is important for the Church and individual Christians

- Explain what the local church does in the local community and why, including reference to a source of wisdom and authority

- Describe the impact the local church has on the individual believer and the local area

- Explain the role and importance of the Church in the worldwide community

- Explain why the Church works for reconciliation

- Describe the problems faced by the persecuted Church

- Give different Christians responses to teachings about charity, with reference to a source of wisdom and authority

- Describe the work of Christian Aid – what it does and why.

Exam practice

On these exam practice pages you will see example answers for each of the exam question types: **a**, **b**, **c**, and **d**. You can find out more about these on pages 6–10.

• Question 'a'

*Question **a** is AO1 – this tests your knowledge and understanding.*

> (a)   Outline **three** Christian sacraments. (3)

Student response

Baptism, bread and wine, becoming a priest

Improved student response

Baptism, formally becoming a member of the Christian Church.

Eucharist, a re-enactment of the last supper.

Holy Orders, becoming a priest, deacon or bishop in Catholic and Orthodox Churches.

 Over to you! Give yourself three minutes on the clock and have a go at answering this question. Remember, this question type requires you to provide three facts or short ideas: you don't need to explain them or express any opinions.

✓ **WHAT WENT WELL**

This student can identify three different types of sacrament.

! **HOW TO IMPROVE**

To make the response clearer and gain full marks the student should use the religious names for the sacraments and explain each one. See the 'improved student response' opposite for suggested corrections.

• Question 'b'

*Question **b** is AO1 – this tests your knowledge and understanding.*

> (b)   Explain **two** reasons why prayer is important to Christians. (4)

Student response

Prayer is important to Christians because it is a way of communicating with God. People can pray for different things, for example, to ask for something.

Improved student response

Prayer is important to Christians because it is a way of communicating with God. Through prayer Christians can give thanks and praise to God but also ask for things on behalf of themselves or others.

Prayer is important to Christians because Jesus taught people to pray using the Lord's Prayer and people like to follow his example. In addition, using formal prayers or words from Church history help Christians to feel a shared sense of belief and unity making this form of prayer important for Christians.

 Over to you! Give yourself four minutes on the clock and have a go at answering this question. Remember, in order to 'explain' something, you need to **develop** your points. See page 9 for a reminder of how to do this.

✓ **WHAT WENT WELL**

This is a low-level response with two vague and basic reasons given. The student correctly identifies that prayer is a way of communicating with God.

 ! **HOW TO IMPROVE**

The reasons given are basic and are not developed. For a high level response students should explain why prayer is important to individual Christians, using examples of how they pray and the types of prayer they use. See the 'improved student response' opposite for suggested corrections.

• Question 'c'

*Question **c** is AO1 – this tests your knowledge and understanding.*

> (c) Explain **two** reasons why giving to charity is important to Christians.
> In your answer you must refer to a source of wisdom and authority. (5)

Student response

The Bible says that Christians must give charity to those in need. Supporting charities is a good thing and the Christian Church seeks to have a positive impact on the world.

Improved student response

Giving to charity is important to Christians because the Bible says that Christians must give charity to those in need. In Jesus' teaching of the parable of the sheep and the goats Jesus says that if we help others, in fact we are helping him, showing that charity to others is important: "whatever you did for one of the least of these brothers and sisters of mine, you did for me" (Matthew 25: 40).

Secondly, Christians are taught that the most charitable act is love and often Christians do not give financially to charity but will give time, effort and skills because supporting charities is a good thing and the Christian Church seeks to have a positive impact on the world.

 Over to you! Give yourself five minutes on the clock and have a go at answering this question. Remember, you need to write two developed points, one of which needs to be supported by a source of wisdom and authority.

 WHAT WENT WELL

This student understands that charity is important and the global Church has a responsibility to help others.

 HOW TO IMPROVE

The link between helping others by giving to charity and Christian teachings on charity could be clearer. Has the student included a source of wisdom and authority? See the 'improved student response' opposite for suggested corrections.

• Question 'd'

*Question **d** is AO2 – this tests your ability to evaluate. Some d questions also carry an extra three marks for spelling, punctuation and grammar.*

> **In this question, 3 of the marks awarded will be for your spelling, punctuation and grammar and your use of specialist terminology.**
>
> *(d) 'Every Christian should go on a pilgrimage.' Evaluate this statement considering arguments for and against. In your response you should:
> • refer to Christian teachings
> • refer to different Christian points of view
> • reach a justified conclusion. (15)

Student response

Christians have been going on <u>pilgrimiges</u> for centuries, and today <u>pilgrimige</u> is still popular. <u>Pilgrimige</u> can increase a Christian's faith, help them feel closer to God, and may bring about religious experiences.

I would agree with the claim that every Christian should go on a <u>pilgrimige</u>, because it's a spiritual journey towards God. Many popular sites of <u>pilgrimige</u> –

for instance Jerusalem – are visited by Christians and it could be argued that Christians should go to Jerusalem because Jesus himself did this.

However, not all Christians place emphasis on pilgrimige. It might be encouraged as a special opportunity to pray and reflect, but it's not considered to be central to living the Christian life. These Christians might choose to focus on other aspects of their faith instead.

In conclusion, whilst pilgrimige would be very beneficial to all Christians, it's not possible to say that all Christians should go on a pilgrimige. It's not a religious requirement, and in some churches it's not a significant part of the Christian life.

Improved student response

Christians have been going on pilgrimages for centuries, and today pilgrimage is still popular. Pilgrimage can increase a Christian's faith, help them feel closer to God, and may bring about religious experiences.

A member of the Catholic Church could agree with the claim that every Christian should go on a pilgrimage, because the Catholic Church teaches about its importance in the Catechism: 'Pilgrimages evoke our earthly journey toward heaven' (CCC 2691). In other words, pilgrimage is a spiritual journey towards God.

Pilgrimage is important in Protestant churches too, and many popular sites of pilgrimage – for instance Jerusalem and Walsingham – are visited by all denominations. Walsingham, for instance, has Catholic, Anglican, and Orthodox shrines. It could be argued that all Christians should go on a pilgrimage to Jerusalem because Jesus himself did this at the age of twelve and said that he had to be in his Father's house (Luke 2: 49). Pilgrimage can allow Christians to walk in the very footsteps of Jesus, or a saint. Pilgrimage is spiritually important because the pilgrim can, for a moment, be where Jesus or a saint was, see what they saw, and experience what the world was like for them – it makes it special for the pilgrim and something which they will never forget.

However, not all Protestant churches place emphasis on pilgrimage. It might be encouraged as a special opportunity to pray and reflect, but it's not considered to be central to living the Christian life. These Christians might choose to focus on other aspects of their faith instead, for example prayer, Bible study or evangelism – all of which bring Christians closer to God in an everyday way which fits into their lives.

In conclusion, whilst pilgrimage would be very beneficial to all Christians, it's not possible to say that all Christians should go on a pilgrimage. It's not a religious requirement, and in some churches it's not a significant part of the Christian life.

 Over to you! Give yourself 15 minutes on the clock and have a go at answering this question. Remember to refer back to the original statement in your writing when you give different points of view, and make sure you cover each of the bullet points given in the question. Allow three minutes to check your spelling, punctuation and grammar and use of specialist terminology.

 WHAT WENT WELL

This is a mid-level response. The student understands that they must give two opposing sides of the argument and reach a conclusion. They explain both arguments and present a conclusion.

 HOW TO IMPROVE

This student has consistently misspelt the word 'pilgrimage', which would cost them marks. To achieve a high level answer, the student would need to be more specific when referring to different Christian viewpoints, and provide more detail on Christian teachings. See the 'improved student response' opposite for suggested corrections.

 BUILD YOUR SKILLS

In your exams, you'll need to make sure you use religious terminology correctly. Do you know the meaning of the following important terms for this topic?

worship

liturgical

non-liturgical

prejudice

pilgrimage

Advent

Holy Week

mission

evangelism

ecumenism

persecution

Chapter 4:
Equality

4.1 Human rights

What are human rights?

Human rights are the basic rights and freedoms that all human beings are entitled to. Around the world, these rights and freedoms are seen as so important that they are set down in legal declarations and agreements. The intention is that every person should have the same rights as everyone else.

The Universal Declaration of Human Rights was the first global agreement to set out rights for all human beings and it was adopted by the United Nations in 1948. Over 50 member states of the United Nations were involved in writing it; 48 nations voted in favour of adopting the final draft, none voted against, and eight abstained (decided not to vote either for or against).

Some of the key human rights defined in the Universal Declaration include:

> ❝ All human beings are born free and equal in dignity and rights.
> Everyone has the right to life, liberty and security of person.
> No one shall be subjected to torture or to cruel, inhuman or degrading treatment or punishment.
> Everyone is entitled to a fair tribunal [trial] …
> No one shall be subjected to arbitrary interference with his privacy, family, home or correspondence …
> Everyone has the right to freedom of thought, conscience and religion …
> Everyone has the right to freedom of opinion and expression … ❞
> *(Universal Declaration of Human Rights)*

The European Convention on Human Rights (ECHR) is an international treaty that came into force in 1953 to protect human rights in Europe. It is upheld in the UK by the Human Rights Act 1998.

The ECHR defines a range of **obligations**, rights, freedoms and **prohibitions**. Any citizen of a country that signed the ECHR who feels that their rights have been **violated** can take their claim to the European Court of Human Rights. The Convention guarantees many rights for all citizens, including:

- The right to liberty and security
- Prohibition of **discrimination** on any ground such as sex, race, religion
- The right to life
- Freedom of expression
- The right to education
- The right to respect for private and family life.

SPECIFICATION FOCUS

Christian teaching on human rights: Christian teachings and responses to the nature, history and purpose of human rights; the importance of human rights, and why Christians might support them, including Proverbs 14: 31; divergent Christian responses to the need for and application of individual human rights, including the support offered by situation ethics; Christian responses to non-religious (including atheist and Humanist) arguments about human rights.

USEFUL TERMS

Discrimination: treating people less favourably because of an irrelevant factor

Obligation: something that you must do; a responsibility

Prohibition: something that is not allowed to happen

Violate: to break a law or agreement

Imagine what it would be like not having the right to an education. How would that affect your life now and in the future? **SUPPORT**

What real-life examples can you find in recent news reports of human rights violations? Were they in the UK or elsewhere in the world? **STRETCH**

Christian teachings on human rights

Christians often make choices about right and wrong after consulting sources of wisdom and authority. These include the Bible and the words of Jesus, the teachings of the Church and guidance from priests or key Christian thinkers. Christians may also consult their own conscience.

The Bible teaches Christians that 'God created mankind in his own image' (*Genesis 1: 27*) and that all human beings are equally special to him (*Galatians 3: 28*). Christians believe that God gave instructions on how people should treat each other in the Ten Commandments (*Exodus 20: 3–17*) and through the teachings of Jesus in the Sermon on the Mount (*Matthew 5–7*). Key teachings include:

- You shall not murder.
- You shall not commit adultery.
- You shall not steal.
- You shall not give false testimony against your neighbour.

(Exodus 20)

- Love your neighbour as yourself (*Matthew 22: 39*).
- Love your enemies (*Matthew 5: 44*).
- Give to the poor, and you will have treasure in heaven (*Matthew 19: 21*).

These Christian values are the basis of many of today's human rights provisions.

Why might Christians support human rights?

> ❝Whoever oppresses the poor shows contempt for their Maker, but **whoever is kind to the needy honours God.** ❞
> *(Proverbs 14: 31)*

Christians support human rights because:

- Life is holy and belongs to God (the 'sanctity of life')
- Everyone is made in the image of God and should be treated equally
- Freedom of speech, assembly and worship are an essential part of Christianity.

A How should Christians in the UK respond to children living in poverty?

Adultery: a couple having sex even though one (or both) of them is married to someone else **SUPPORT**

False testimony: telling lies

How do these obligations compare with the human rights listed on page 110? **STRETCH**

 CASE STUDY: WORLD VISION

We are Christian
We follow the teachings of Jesus who calls us to love our neighbours, care for children and challenge injustice.

We are committed to the poor
We are called to serve the neediest people of the earth, to relieve their suffering and to promote the transformation of their well-being.

We value people
We believe that every person is created equal and entitled to freedom, justice, peace and opportunity. We celebrate the richness of diversity in human personality, culture and contribution.

How is this organisation motivated by Christianity? **SUPPORT** Can you link some of these ideas to Christian teachings?

World Vision ®

What are divergent Christian responses to the need for and application of human rights?

Many people in the UK, including Christians, argue that Christian values should not be imposed on the secular government. Indeed, in the Bible, St Paul tells Christians that they should obey political leaders because authority has been given to them by God (*Romans 13: 1*).

The Christian Church in the UK supports human rights laws therefore. However, within church practice there is a degree of diversity based on the interpretation of teachings in the Bible:

- The Catholic Church allows men to become priests, but not women.
- Some Protestant churches do not allow female or homosexual priests.
- Some churches overseas, particularly in Africa, are opposed to certain rights for homosexuals.

Situation ethics

Situation ethics is an ethical theory first suggested by an American scholar called Joseph Fletcher. When he first proposed the theory he was a member of the Episcopelian Church. Situation ethics says that the only rule that should be followed is: in any situation do the most loving action. This is why it is called *situation* ethics. Fletcher claimed that all other rules, and other moral demands like human rights, can be overridden if this is the more loving thing to do. For this reason, situation ethics could be seen to be in support of some human rights in some situations, but overall situation ethics does not accept any absolute moral standards such as human rights.

For instance, Joseph Fletcher supported the bombing of Hiroshima in 1945, even though it was contrary to the rights of all the innocent civilians killed, because it brought about the end of the Second World War. He argued that the greater good of ending the war was worth more than the lives lost in the bombing – so this was, in his view, the most loving action in the situation.

How do Christians respond to non-religious arguments about human rights?

Atheist and Humanist arguments

Even though **atheists** and **Humanists** don't have a set of 'teachings' compiled together as a source of authority, human rights is still of vital importance. Within atheism there is a range of views based on the idea that, if there is no God, a person must decide for themselves how to treat other human beings. Most atheists would decide to do the most helpful or beneficial thing for society.

Humanists are committed to the protection and promotion of human rights, as representative of shared human needs. They are often involved in campaigns for equal rights for homosexuals and ethnic minorities, and support for people living in poor nations.

USEFUL TERMS

Atheist: someone who does not believe in the existence of God

Humanist: a non-religious person who looks to reason and empathy in order to live a meaningful life

Situation ethics: ethical decisions are made according to the specific context of the decision

Do you think Fletcher's reasoning in this situation **STRETCH** was sound? Why or why not? How might a Christian respond today?

B The aftermath of one of the terrorist bombings in London on 7 July 2005. Would lethal action against bombers be justified?

'For Humanists, living our lives well means trying to increase human happiness and well-being in this world, and to help lessen suffering and unhappiness [...] We should do this for the benefit of humanity.'
British Humanist Association

Christian responses

Human rights are important to Christians, atheists and Humanists alike, so many Christians would affirm the good work of atheists and Humanists. For example, the Church of England has affirmed the 'positive beliefs' held within Humanism.

However, the Church of England has also highlighted 'fundamental differences in purpose and outlook'. The purpose of the Church is primarily about the work of God: Christians obey the teachings of the Bible because they believe that God loves and cares for humanity and calls Christians to join with him in bringing healing. By contrast, atheists and Humanists do not believe in a higher power.

 C People gather at Ascot to watch and place bets on horse racing

BUILD YOUR SKILLS

1   a   What is the purpose of humans rights?
    b   Do you think they are important? Why/why not?

2   Why would a Christian be against the following? Refer to specific Christian teachings.
    a   A business owner who pays below the minimum wage.
    b   A member of another faith being bullied for their beliefs.

3   Look at images **A** and **C**. Answer the following questions.
    a   What human rights are these people benefiting from?
    b   Have they been denied any human rights? If so, which?
    c   How do you think the people in image C should react to the family in image A?
    d   What conclusions do you draw from these images?

4   What is the main difference between non-religious and Christian approaches to human rights? Would this impact the nature of a person's response to human rights violations? Explain your views. **STRETCH**

SUMMARY

- Most people believe that everyone is entitled to basic human rights.
- Many societies think human rights are so important that they are protected by national laws and international agreements.
- Many Christians believe that understanding of God and his love of humanity underpins human rights.
- Humanists believe human rights exist for the benefit of humanity.

? EXAM-STYLE QUESTIONS

a   Outline **three** Christian teachings that relate to human rights. (3)

d   'Human rights should always be observed.'
Evaluate this statement considering arguments for and against. In your response you should:
- refer to Christian teachings
- refer to different Christian points of view
- reach a justified conclusion. (12)

4.2 Equality

What problems are caused by inequality?

Inequality can occur when people make decisions about others without necessarily taking into account all the facts – for example, when they act on their belief that men are superior to women. Inequality can occur between individuals, but it can also be very far-reaching, for instance economic inequality between two different nations.

There are many types of inequality in the world, including inequalities between:

- men and women
- races
- ethnic and national groups
- people with and without disabilities
- rich and poor
- people of different ages
- people who use different languages.

These inequalities can mean that people have unequal access to:

- food
- education
- health
- liberty and security
- life opportunities
- employment
- housing
- money.

Inequalities can create feelings of resentment and injustice, potentially causing conflict at personal, local, national and international level.

SPECIFICATION FOCUS

Christian attitudes towards equality: Christian teachings and responses to the causes of inequality and problems caused by inequality in the world; Christian teachings about equality, including Galatians 3: 23–29; possible solutions and the reasons for them.

B A protest march in London about the problems mothers face in Britain. What is this particular person demonstrating about?

MOST MOTHERS EARN £5.73. TRY RAISING A FAMILY ON THAT!

A A protest march in London about government cuts to disability benefits and services. In what ways might these people have experienced inequality?

The Hardest Hit

What does Christianity teach about equality?

Christianity teaches that everyone is equal in God's eyes. Christians believe that they should treat everyone with love. The Bible says:

> ❛A new commandment I give you: Love one another. As I have loved you, so you must love one another.❜
> *(John 13: 34)*

> ❛Love your neighbour as yourself.❜
> *(Matthew 22: 39)*

Another important teaching in Christianity is that Jesus came to make all people 'children of God':

> ❛So in Christ Jesus you are all children of God through faith, for all of you who were baptised into Christ have clothed yourselves with Christ. **There is neither Jew nor Gentile, neither slave nor free, nor is there male and female, for you are all one in Christ Jesus.** If you belong to Christ, then you are Abraham's seed, and heirs according to the promise.❜
> *(Galatians 3: 26–28)*

A **Gentile** is a person who is not Jewish. At the time Galatians was written, there were some conflicts between Jews and Gentiles. **SUPPORT**

How does this teaching link to the covenant with Abraham? (see 2.1) **STRETCH**

This teaching says that, under Jesus, the factors that used to separate people are replaced by a new unity.

Many Christians have followed Christian teachings to try and improve equality in the world. For instance, the Archbishop of York, John Sentamu, used the Parable of the Good Samaritan to show how Jesus taught his followers to treat everyone equally. He used himself as an example to raise awareness of racial inequality – there are not many black bishops in the Church of England.

In 1985, the Church of England published 'Faith in the City', a report highlighting the need for governments to be concerned about the poor and needy in the towns and cities of the UK.

> ❛God […] is also to be found, despite all appearances, in the apparent waste lands of our inner cities and housing estates: that men and women are created to glorify God in and through his creation and to serve fellow human beings in the power of his love.❜
> *(Faith in the City)*

C Archbishop John Sentamu, right, with Archbishop Justin Welby

What are the solutions to inequality?

Ways of tackling inequality could include:

- making unequal treatment illegal – for example, the Equality Act 2010 makes it illegal to treat women and men differently in employment and education
- promoting and encouraging good community relations to encourage people to work together
- getting to know people from other backgrounds to develop friendship and greater understanding
- being aware of inequality and changing situations to avoid it
- changing people's attitudes through education, to get at the root of the problem
- increasing awareness of the treatment of minority groups so that marginalised people are given a voice.

All forms of discrimination go against the United Nations Declaration of Human Rights: **STRETCH**

> ❛ Article 2. Everyone is entitled to all the rights and freedoms set forth in this Declaration, without distinction of any kind, such as race, colour, sex, language, religion, political or other opinion, national or social origin, property, birth or other status. ❜

D This is a washing label in the back of a T-shirt. Should labels like this be banned, in your opinion? Why/why not?

BUILD YOUR SKILLS

1 What is **equality**? Write a definition in your own words.

2 Copy and complete the following table for four causes of inequality:

Cause	Possible solution	How should Christians respond?

3 'Sometimes, inequality is unavoidable.'   **STRETCH**
   a List arguments for and against this statement, including reference to Christian teachings.
   b Make notes on each argument about how convincing they are.
   c Plan an essay which evaluates the statement using the arguments. You'll also need to plan what you'll say in your conclusion.

SUMMARY

- There are many types of inequality in the world.
- Christianity supports equal rights for all because the Bible teaches that all people are equal in God's eyes.
- Solutions to inequality could include making unequal treatment illegal and encouraging good community relations.

EXAM-STYLE QUESTIONS

a Outline **three** solutions to inequality. (3)
b Explain **two** reasons why living in an equal society is important for Christians. (4)

4.3 Religious freedom

What is religious freedom?

Religious freedom means people's right to practise their religion and to change their religion – they are free to follow any religion they choose, or none.

The UK is a multi-faith society, where many different religious groups live together in one society. This means:

- people of different religious faiths or none live alongside each other
- all faiths have an equal right to co-exist (religious pluralism)
- followers of all religions are free to worship.

The Census report for 2011 gave the numbers of people who identified themselves as followers of different religions in England and Wales as follows:

- Christian – 33 million
- Muslim – 2.7 million
- Hindu – 800,000
- Jewish – 263,000
- Buddhist – 245,000
- No religion – 14 million

SPECIFICATION FOCUS

Christian attitudes towards religious freedom: Christian teachings and responses to the nature of religious freedom, including reference to the Catechism of the Catholic Church 1738 and 1747; the response of the Church to a multi-faith society; the benefits and challenges for Christians living in a multi-faith society; Christian responses to non-religious arguments (including atheist and Humanist) against aspects of religious freedom.

How do Christians respond to religious freedom?

Christians accept religious freedom because they believe that God gives people free will to choose whether or not to believe in him. Christians therefore would affirm the right of everyone to choose for themselves which faith to follow, or none. However, whilst believing this is the case, many Christians also believe that they should tell others about their faith. Christians approach this matter differently:

- **Religious inclusivism** – the belief that Christianity is completely right and other religions have only part of the truth. Christians should respect other religions, but their followers should be encouraged to become Christians. This is largely the view of the Catholic Church and many Protestant Churches.
- **Religious exclusivism** – the belief that only Christianity is right and all other religions are wrong. Christians should actively invite followers of other faiths, or none, to convert to Christianity. This is the view of many evangelical Protestant Churches.
- Some Christians believe that people may follow whatever religion they wish, or not be religious at all, and will not try to invite others to convert to Christianity. This is the view of more liberal Protestant Churches.

This is quite a rare meeting of the world's religious leaders in 2011. Do you think that they should meet more or less often? Why? **STRETCH**

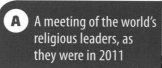

A A meeting of the world's religious leaders, as they were in 2011

117

Some people argue that, as the UK is a Christian country in the main, Christian traditions (such as Christmas) and moral rules should be given first priority. Christmas is a national holiday for everyone in the UK. No other religion has a national holiday for their special days.

To promote religious harmony, several national groups have been set up:

- the Inter Faith Network for the UK – founded in 1987 to promote good relations between people of different faiths
- local groups include inter-faith groups in Leeds, Cambridge and Glasgow
- individual churches often have local links with other faith groups and meet regularly.

Some churches have also declared their support for religious harmony. For example, in September 2006, Pope Benedict XVI expressed his 'profound respect for all Muslims'. The Catechism of the Catholic Church declares:

B Christmas transforms London every year

> ❝Freedom is exercised in relationships between human beings. Every human person, created in the image of God, has the natural right to be recognized as a free and responsible being. All owe to each other this duty of respect. [...] This right must be recognized and protected by civil authority within the limits of the common good and public order.❞
> *(CCC, 1738)*

> ❝The right to the exercise of freedom, especially in religious and moral matters, is an inalienable requirement of the dignity of man. But the exercise of freedom does not entail the putative right to say or do anything.❞
> *(CCC, 1747)*

These quotations say that freedom is a very important part of what it means to be a human being. This doesn't mean, however, that a person is always free to say and do whatever they want – for example, if what they want to do breaks the law or is harmful to others.

SUPPORT

What are the benefits and challenges for Christians living in a multi-faith society?

A multi-faith society can be a benefit to Christians because:

- Christians can get to know people of other faiths and build their understanding of different beliefs
- religious groups from all over the world can work towards living peacefully together
- Christians can find new ways of enjoying life with different people, and may also experience a richer and more varied cultural life
- living in a multi-faith community can promote more friendship and less prejudice.

However, a multi-faith society can also challenge Christians in several ways:

- it can make them think about and question their own faith more deeply
- it may require them to be more open to the views of others
- it may require them to be more tolerant and understanding of other faiths.

Christian responses to non-religious views

Although most non-religious people would agree with the idea of religious freedom, in reality they may disagree with how religious freedom is interpreted, and at what point it infringes on the freedom of others. For example, many non-religious people (including atheists and Humanists) would question how some Christians approach missionary and evangelical work (see 3.6). The British Humanist Association, for example, has questioned the influence of Christianity within education and have spoken out against faith schools and the way they might attempt to 'indoctrinate' young people. Humanists and atheists might also challenge the influence of Christianity in other cultures overseas and the impact it might have on certain communities.

Christian responses to these views will vary, because not all Christians have the same views on mission and evangelism (see page 117). Sharing the gospel with others is a core belief within Christianity and therefore Christians could argue that to practise this is within the bounds of religious freedom, and freedom of expression. Many Christians would aim to share their faith only with those who they believe are receptive to it. Others, however, believe their faith calls them to preach the gospel to all people. Christian teaching affirms the right of the listener to choose whether or not to accept the Christian message.

C Diwali celebrations in the UK

BUILD YOUR SKILLS

1 What is religious freedom? Write a definition.

2 Explain three different Christian approaches to religious freedom in your own words.

3 Why do some Christians and non-religious people disagree about religious freedom? Explain your answer using at least two developed points.

4 'Other faiths should also get a national holiday'. Consider arguments for and against this statement and explain your conclusions. **STRETCH**

SUMMARY

- Religious freedom is a person's right to practise their faith or none.
- Christians affirm religious freedom, though many believe they also have a right to try to convince others to become Christians.
- Some Christians and non-religious people would disagree over some approaches to evangelism.

? EXAM-STYLE QUESTIONS

a Outline **three** ways Christians can approach religious freedom. (3)

b Explain **two** non-religious arguments against aspects of religious freedom. (4)

What are prejudice and discrimination?

- **Prejudice** is the belief that certain people are inferior or superior without having any actual experience of them.

- Prejudice occurs when someone holds an opinion about someone else that is not based on fact – for example, believing that all women are bad drivers or that men can't multi-task.

- Prejudice can relate to differences of religion, race, sex, language, disability, age and many other factors.

- Discrimination means treating people less favourably because of their race, sex, sexual orientation, age, religion or belief, disability, marital status, class or other characteristics.

- Discrimination occurs when people act upon their prejudices without accepting all the facts – for instance, only employing men because they believe without evidence that women cannot do the job.

When people are *prejudiced*, this can lead them to *discriminate* against others and treat them unequally. Prejudice and discrimination can lead to anger, resentment, conflict, and a feeling of deep unfairness.

UK law

The UK, as a multi-faith society, has laws to prevent religious and other discrimination:

- The Racial and Religious Hatred Act 2006 makes it an offence to use threatening words or behaviour to stir up religious hatred.

- The Education Act 2011 requires schools to promote community cohesion.

- The Equality Act 2010 legislates against discrimination on grounds of sex, disability and race.

 SPECIFICATION FOCUS

Christian attitudes to prejudice and discrimination: Christian teachings and responses to the nature of prejudice and discrimination and the problems they cause; Christian teachings on why prejudice and discrimination against religions is wrong, including reference to Galatians 2: 1–10.

 USEFUL TERMS

Prejudice: a belief that someone is inferior or superior without having any actual experience of them

A Throughout history, people have been discriminated against for their faith

What does Christianity teach about prejudice and discrimination?

The Bible teaches that prejudice and discrimination are wrong:

> ‘God does not show favouritism. ’
> *(Galatians 2: 6)*

> ‘There is neither Jew nor Gentile, neither slave nor free, nor is there male and female, for you are all one in Christ Jesus. ’
> *(Galatians 3: 28)*

> ‘So God created mankind in his own image, in the image of God he created them; male and female he created them. ’
> *(Genesis 1: 27)*

> ‘Love your neighbour as yourself. ’
> *(Luke 10: 27)*

Christians believe that people should be treated with equal respect, and many Christians see it as their duty actively to prevent discrimination through inter-faith and charity work, and education.

 B Do signs like this reflect prejudice? Why/why not?

 BUILD YOUR SKILLS

1 a Examine the scenarios outlined below.
- A woman applies for a job which involves carrying heavy loads. She is rejected because she is a woman.
- A black man is refused a job as a waiter in a Chinese restaurant because the restaurant wants a Chinese atmosphere.
- A Muslim is sacked from his job in a supermarket because he is unwilling to handle pork – consumption of pork is forbidden in Islam.
- A wheelchair user is refused a university place because the university does not have accessible facilities.

   b Explain the prejudice and discrimination each scenario presents.
   c How could you use Christian teachings to challenge the prejudice and discrimination in these scenarios?

2 Look at the images labelled **A**. Why do you think that some people discriminate against followers of different religions? **STRETCH**

 SUMMARY

- Prejudice and discrimination cause problems in society.
- Christianity teaches that all people are equally valuable in the eyes of God.
- The UK has legislation to prevent discrimination.

? **EXAM-STYLE QUESTIONS**

b Explain **two** problems caused by prejudice and discrimination. (4)
c Explain **two** Christian beliefs about prejudice and discrimination. In your answer you must refer to a source of wisdom and authority. (5)

4.5 Racial harmony

Racial harmony refers to a situation in which people from different races and cultures live together amicably in one society. The UK is a multi-ethnic society, made up of many different races, cultures and nationalities.

The 2011 Census reported that the following numbers of people in England and Wales identified their ethnicity as:

- White – 43 million
- Asian – 7.5 million
- Black – 3.3 million
- Mixed race – 2.2 million.

Even though there are laws in place to combat **racism**, it is still experienced by people today, and is widely reported in the media (see 4.6).

What does Christianity teach about racial harmony?

The Bible teaches that all races are equal before God:

- 'God created man in his own image.' (*Genesis 1: 27*)
- 'You are all one in Christ.' (*Galatians 3: 28*)
- 'God does not show favouritism, but accepts men from every nation.' (*Acts 10: 34–35*)
- In the Parable of the Good Samaritan (*Luke 10: 25–37*), Jesus taught that people from different races and ethnic groups should not hate each other, but should follow God's command and love their neighbour.

One of the most important of Jesus' teachings was the command for everyone to love one another:

> ❝A new command I give you: **Love one another**. As I have loved you, so you should love one another.❞
> *John 13: 34*

However, what exactly does it mean to 'love one another'? This idea of love comes from the Greek word 'agape', which means unconditional love – that is, one person loves another without conditions – not because they want something from the other person, but just loving them because they are a human being. Love itself, in this context, means 'wanting the best for the other person.'

SPECIFICATION FOCUS

Christian attitudes towards racial harmony: Christian teachings and responses to racial harmony including interpretations of John 13: 34, including links to situation ethics; how and why Christians have worked for racial harmony, including the work and teachings of Desmond Tutu; the benefits for Christians of living in a multi-ethnic society.

USEFUL TERMS

Racial harmony: people from different races and cultures living together amicably in one society

Racism: the belief that some races are inferior to others

Situation ethics

Situation ethics (see 4.1) would demand that in each situation the most loving action should be carried out. With reference to racial harmony, this would usually be to ensure that everyone, whatever their race, should be treated with respect as an expression of love. However, situation ethics doesn't think that any rules or rights apply in all cases, even the moral rules that forbid prejudice and discrimination. But also, situation ethics would encourage disobeying any laws which were not in the best interests of people of all races.

Why should Christians promote racial harmony?

Christian churches throughout the world oppose racism and encourage Christians to treat everyone equally, for example:

- 'Every form of social or cultural discrimination […] must be curbed and eradicated as incompatible with God's design.' (*Catechism of the Catholic Church, 1935*)

- 'The Methodist Church believes that racism is a denial of the gospel.' (*Methodist Conference 2009, motion 203*)

Because of the teachings of the Church and the Bible, Christians work to promote racial harmony.

CASE STUDY: DESMOND TUTU

Desmond Tutu was the first black Archbishop of South Africa. He led a campaign of peaceful protests in an attempt to gain equal status for black people at a time when the country was ruled by white people. Tutu was imprisoned several times, but the campaigns finally succeeded and the racist system known as apartheid – a policy of strict social segregation and discrimination based on race – finally ended in 1994. Tutu said:

> If it weren't for faith, I would have given up long ago. I am certain that lots of us would be hate-filled and bitter … [The Scriptures] speak of a God who … turns you around to be concerned for your neighbour.

Tutu was awarded the Nobel Peace Prize in 1984. In 1996, in recognition of his work within the Church, he received the Archbishop of Canterbury's Award for Outstanding Service to the Anglican Communion.

B Desmond Tutu

C During the apartheid in South Africa, racism was a common experience for black people

CASE STUDY: MARTIN LUTHER KING

In the US, Dr Martin Luther King Jr, a committed Christian, dedicated his life to gaining equal rights for black people, many of whom were badly treated by white people. He organised peaceful protests and in 1964 won the Nobel Peace Prize. Thanks to his work, black people secured equal voting rights in 1965. King was assassinated in 1968.

 Martin Luther King

The benefits of living in a multi-ethnic society

For Christians, living in a multi-ethnic society has many benefits, including:

- The opportunity to get to know people of different races and cultures
- Worshipping together with Christians of other races and cultures and therefore feeling part of a global community of believers
- Enjoying richness of culture including music, food, and celebrations
- The opportunity to be brought together with new people who have fresh ideas.

E Notting Hill Carnival – an important multi-faith and multi-racial event held in London every year

 BUILD YOUR SKILLS

1 Explain the meaning of these two terms: racial harmony, racism.

2 a Make a list of reasons why Christians should promote racial harmony.
  b If a Christian witnesses racist behaviour, what should they do and why? Write a paragraph and refer to a Christian teaching in your answer.

3 Read the quotation from Desmond Tutu. Do you agree with his claim that, without faith, 'lots of us would be hate-filled and bitter'? Explain your reasons. STRETCH

 SUMMARY

- Christianity teaches people to treat everyone equally and to oppose racism.
- Some high-profile Christians who have worked towards racial harmony include Archbishop Desmond Tutu and Dr Martin Luther King Jr.
- The benefits for Christians of living in a multi-ethnic society include building understanding of other people and an enriched cultural life.

? EXAM-STYLE QUESTIONS

b Explain **two** ways that Christians have worked for racial harmony. (4)
c Explain **two** reasons why racial harmony is important to Christians. In your answer you must refer to a source of wisdom and authority. (5)

4.6 Racial discrimination

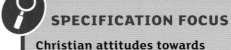

SPECIFICATION FOCUS

Christian attitudes towards racial discrimination: Christian teachings and responses to racial discrimination; how and why racial discrimination causes problems in society, including Acts 17: 22–28.

How does Christianity respond to racial discrimination?

As we have seen in 4.5, Christian teachings oppose racial discrimination. As in all things, the Christian response to racial discrimination is based on the model that Jesus himself presents. Jesus' attitude to all of humanity was one of love. For example, there is a racial element to the parable of the Good Samaritan (*Luke 10*), which teaches that people should help anyone in need, no matter who they are. In Jesus' day, Samaritans were regarded as second class citizens by many Jews. Jesus (a Jew) also accepts and brings comfort and guidance to a Samaritan woman (*John 4*) which would have been wholly condemned at the time.

Given the example set by Jesus, it might be expected that the early Church would follow this pattern, but the reality is that the early Christians struggled. *Acts 6* shows there was a dispute because the Jewish followers of Jesus were neglecting the Greek widows in favour of the Jewish widows when distributing food. The disciples had to take action to rectify this. *Acts 10* shows Peter's struggle to go and preach to Cornelius' household because Cornelius was a Roman. The *Acts 10* narrative describes how God had to remind Peter in a dream that he didn't discriminate and Peter shouldn't either.

By *Acts 15*, the dispute between the early followers of Jesus was such that a special gathering had to be held in Jerusalem to discuss who exactly could be a follower of Jesus and what rules they would have to follow. The ruling of Jerusalem was clear: all could become followers of Jesus. It would be this ruling that would empower Paul and other disciples to continue to extend the message of Jesus beyond the Jews. An example can be seen in *Acts 17*, when Paul stands in front of a gathered crowd in Athens. Jesus' words were now being carried to Jews, Romans, and Greeks, and would soon be heard across the whole world.

> ❝From one man he made all the nations, that they should inhabit the whole earth...❞
> *(Acts 17: 26)*

A A barbecue in 1930s Alabama, US, showing racial segregation; African-American and white people are separated by a long counter

The UK law on racial discrimination

Section 9 of the Equality Act 2010 makes it unlawful to discriminate on grounds of colour, nationality and ethnic or national origins.

What problems does racial discrimination cause in society?

Racial discrimination can occur in many forms, for example:

- racist employers may not give jobs to certain people
- racist landlords may refuse accommodation to certain groups
- racist people may make abusive remarks.

Racism is the belief that certain racial or ethnic groups are inferior or superior to others. This attitude can lead to discrimination, persecution and the violation of human rights. It creates serious problems in society:

- inequality and injustice
- lack of opportunity
- resentment and anger
- unrest and conflict.

Such feelings of injustice can escalate from a sense of personal grievance and conflict between individuals, to civil unrest, which can all stir up more hatred in turn.

One area of concern regarding racism and equality in society is the disproportionately low numbers of people from black and minority ethnic groups in professional and public sectors, for example: in the police force and legal system, at top business management level, and politicians and senior civil servants.

B There are low numbers of black and minority ethnic officers in the police force

In the past, single acts of racism have triggered riots. Why do you think this can happen? **STRETCH**

C The 'stop and search' of black teenagers has caused controversy in the media

BUILD YOUR SKILLS

1   Examine the examples of racial discrimination below. Explain how Christian teachings could be applied to each of these situations.
    - A group of black teenagers are repeatedly stopped and searched by police.
    - An employer does not employ any workers from overseas because he believes that British workers are best.
    - An elderly white woman objects to being treated by 'foreign' nurses.
    - A white bus driver orders a young black woman to give up her seat so that an elderly white woman can sit down.

2   Why do you think there are disproportionately low numbers of black and minority ethnic groups in professional and public sectors? Is anything being done to combat this? **STRETCH**

SUMMARY

- Christianity teaches that discrimination on the grounds of race is wrong.
- In UK law, racial discrimination is wrong.
- Serious problems can occur when people are discriminated against.

? EXAM-STYLE QUESTIONS

a   Outline **three** problems caused by racial discrimination. (3)

b   Explain **two** reasons why Christians should combat racial discrimination. (4)

4.7 Social justice

What is social justice?

Social justice is about transforming people's lives by restoring equality and human rights – especially the lives of those who are most in need. In 2012, the UK government published a plan called 'Social Justice: transforming lives' which aimed to mend 'broken Britain', tackle poverty, and in particular to change the lives of those with multiple disadvantages forever.

At that time in the UK:

- 2.67 million people were unemployed
- 3.8 million children were living in poverty
- 50 per cent of young black males were unemployed.

Despite successful initiatives led by churches and other groups, like the Social Action & Research Foundation, the overall picture in the UK is very similar today.

How are wealth and opportunity distributed in the UK and around the world?

In the UK, wealth is not evenly distributed. In 2014, the Office for National Statistics reported that:

- The UK's richest 1 per cent have more money between them than the poorest 55 per cent put together
- Wealth in the south-east of England rises five times faster than in the rest of the UK
- One in nine families has a second home or rental property
- The five richest families in the UK have the same amount of wealth as 12 million ordinary people put together.

Rachel Orr, the head of poverty at the charity Oxfam called the poverty figures:

> 6 a shocking chapter in a tale of two Britains [...] it cannot be right that in Britain today a small elite are getting richer and richer while millions are struggling to make ends meet. 9

The situation world-wide is similar. The Credit Suisse Global Report 2014 reported that:

- The richest 1 per cent of the world's population own 48 per cent of the world's wealth.
- The poor in the world own only 1 per cent of the world's wealth.
- The richest 85 people in the world have more money than the poorest 3.5 billion people put together.

SPECIFICATION FOCUS

Christian attitudes to social justice: Christian teachings and responses to the nature and history of the distribution of wealth and opportunity in the UK and the world; Christian teachings about social justice, including reference to Matthew 25: 31–46, and the way the Church works for social justice, including links to situation ethics.

USEFUL TERMS

Social justice: restoring equality and human rights to those in need, especially in relation to unfair distribution of wealth and opportunity

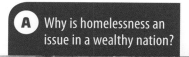

A Why is homelessness an issue in a wealthy nation?

Christian responses to the distribution of wealth and opportunity

The Bible contains many teachings about the poor – sometimes addressing poor people directly, and at other times advising others on how to care for the poor. Examples of beliefs and teachings are as follows:

Christian belief	Teaching
God comforts and defends the poor	❛He defends the cause of the fatherless and the widow, and loves the foreigner residing among you, giving them food and clothing.❜ *(Deuteronomy 10: 17–18)*
The poor are given special honour by God	❛Blessed are you who are poor, for yours is the kingdom of God.❜ *(Luke 6: 20–21)*
People must speak up on behalf of the poor	❛Speak up for those who cannot speak for themselves, for the rights of all who are destitute. Speak up and judge fairly; defend the rights of the poor and needy.❜ *(Proverbs 31: 8–9)*
People must give generously to the poor	❛Give generously to them and do so without a grudging heart...❜ *(Deuteronomy 15: 10–11)*

Some Christian groups put such principles into action in a variety of practical ways; others take a more political approach.

CASE STUDY: CHURCH ACTION ON POVERTY

Church Action on Poverty is a 'national ecumenical Christian social justice charity, committed to tackling poverty in the UK':

❛For Christians [...] the gap is an affront to God who made all human beings of equal worth. The churches have a theological and biblical duty to express the need to close the gap [...] Christianity, like politics, is to be concerned for the welfare of all...❜

❛We want to see significant changes in policy and practice, including: action to reduce tax avoidance and evasion; fairer employment (with public bodies and churches paying the Living Wage); better access to affordable credit; and a reduction in the 'poverty premium'. We will work to achieve this through lobbying, campaigning and social media.❜

B Church Action on Poverty's 'End Hunger Fast' campaign in 2014; many Christians fasted for days during Lent to raise awareness of the hunger crisis in the UK and the growing use of food banks

What is the 'gap'? Why does this organisation call the gap an 'affront' (offence) to God? **SUPPORT**

What does Christianity teach about social justice?

❝A new command I give you: Love one another. As I have loved you, so you should love one another.❞
(John 13: 34)

❝The King will reply, 'Truly I tell you, whatever you did for one of the least of these brothers and sisters of mine, you did for me.❞
(Matthew 25: 40)

C Refugees and migrants protesting in Calais

This passage, from the parable of the sheep and goats, underlines the idea that God wants people to help the most vulnerable members of society as if they were helping Jesus. Christians therefore ought to approach social justice with a special sense of importance. Some examples of Christians today achieving this are:

- The London Churches Refugee Fund provides basic needs such as food and medicine.
- Church Action on Poverty campaigns for justice for the poor.
- The Archbishop's Council campaigns to highlight problems of social injustice.
- The Salvation Army offers shelter, help and advice to needy people.

Situation ethics

Situation ethics would teach that in each situation we should do what is most loving. In many cases it would line up with Jesus' teaching in *Matthew 25*, since the most loving thing to do would be to feed the hungry, clothe the naked and welcome the stranger, for example. Situation ethics would also allow you to break the law in order to help the poor and needy because it does not believe any rules apply at all times and in all places.

> **STRETCH**
>
> According to situation ethics, decisions should be made based on the most loving thing in the circumstances. What would be the most loving thing to do in this situation? How could someone disagree with you?

BUILD YOUR SKILLS

1   Examine the examples of modern social injustice issues below. How do you think **a** Christian teachings and **b** situation ethics could be used to help resolve these situations?
   - a group of migrants protest after they are searched by police.
   - a wealthy person jumps the queue by paying for hospital treatment privately, so a poorer person has to wait longer.
   - a Christian walks past a street beggar who is asking for money for food.

SUMMARY

- Social justice is about transforming lives by restoring equality and human rights to those in need.
- In the UK and throughout the world, wealth is not evenly distributed.
- Christians and Christian organisations campaign for social justice.

EXAM-STYLE QUESTIONS

b   Explain **two** reasons why social injustice can cause problems. (4)

d   'All Christians have a duty to help the most vulnerable members of society.'
Evaluate this statement considering arguments for and against. In your response you should:
   - refer to Christian teachings
   - refer to relevant ethical arguments
   - reach a justified conclusion. (12)

4.8 Wealth and poverty

The nature and causes of poverty

As we have seen in 4.7, wealth in the UK and in the world is unevenly distributed. This means that there are people around the world living in poverty. Poverty is caused by a wide range of factors. In the UK, it may be caused by:

- unemployment – leading to depression, debt and low self-worth
- low pay – leading to poor housing and lifestyle
- lack of education – leading to difficulty in finding good jobs
- homelessness – it is difficult to get a job without having an address
- social background – those born into wealthy families are less likely to experience poverty than those born into poor families.

Around the world, in developing countries and some developed countries, poverty may be caused by similar factors as in the UK, but also:

- climate
- famine
- disease (for example, HIV)
- the lack of clean water
- war – a government's money may be spent on weapons rather than food for the poor and people may be displaced because of fighting
- corruption – leaders may not distribute resources fairly
- unfair trading – traders may not receive a fair price for their goods
- natural disasters – earthquakes and famines can be devastating.

There are two types of poverty:

SPECIFICATION FOCUS

Christian attitudes towards wealth and poverty: Christian teachings and responses to the nature and causes of poverty in the UK and in the world including absolute and relative; Christian teachings about wealth and poverty, including biblical examples such as Matthew 25: 31–47 and links to virtue ethics.

USEFUL TERMS

Absolute poverty: a severe lack of basic human necessities, e.g. food, clean water, sanitation, shelter, education, and health care

Relative poverty: being significantly worse off than the majority of the population

Virtue ethics: an ethical theory that emphasises character and morality above merely obeying rules

Absolute poverty – a severe lack of basic human necessities – food, clean water, sanitation, shelter, education, and health care. This is the worst kind of poverty and is mainly found in undeveloped countries. It is not generally found in developed countries.

A Absolute poverty

Relative poverty – some people are significantly worse off than the majority of the population. This is more commonly found in developed countries.

B Relative poverty – can you see the difference?

What Biblical teachings are there about wealth and poverty?

The Golden Rule

Jesus taught that helping the poor is one of the most important things that a Christian can do. Indeed, it forms the basis of the 'Golden Rule' which holds that you should do to others what you would want them to do for you. In *Matthew 25: 35–36*, Jesus teaches that Christians have a duty to care for the needy – it is as if, when serving the poor, they are serving Jesus himself.

> ❝For I was hungry and you gave me something to eat, I was thirsty and you gave me something to drink, I was a stranger and you invited me in, I needed clothes and you clothed me, I was sick and you looked after me, I was in prison and you came to visit me.❞
> *(Matthew 25: 35–36)*

The Bible teaches that it is easy for money to become a priority, and cause people to forget God, and the needs of other people.

> ❝For where your treasure is, there your heart will also be.❞
> *(Matthew 6: 21)*

> ❝Keep your lives free from the love of money.❞
> *(Hebrews 13: 5)*

> ❝For the love of money is the root of all kinds of evil.❞
> *(1 Timothy 6: 10)*

Virtue ethics

The above teachings link to **virtue ethics**, which is an ethical theory that emphasises character and morality above merely obeying commands. Although there are commands in the Bible about helping the poor and needy, emphasis is placed on the heart (the virtue of the person who carries out the action). Jesus challenges hypocrisy in the context of giving (*Matthew 6: 2*), which means that the inner morality of the person ought to match the action they carry out.

 C How does this action comply with Christian teachings?

 BUILD YOUR SKILLS

1 a What are the two types of poverty and how are they different?
  b What are the causes of poverty in the UK?

2 What does the Bible teach about wealth? Write a paragraph explaining, referring to at least two teachings.

EXAM-STYLE QUESTIONS

b Explain **two** different types of poverty. (4)

d 'It is wrong to be wealthy.' Evaluate this statement considering arguments for and against. In your response you should:
  • refer to Christian teachings
  • reach a justified conclusion. (12)

 SUMMARY

- Poverty in the UK is caused by a wide range of factors, including unemployment, low pay, and social background, and in the wider world it can also include factors such as climate, famine, and unfair trading.
- There are two kinds of poverty: **absolute** (a severe lack of basic necessities) and **relative** (being worse off than the majority of the population).
- The Bible teaches that helping the poor is one of the most important duties of a Christian.

Revision

BUILD YOUR SKILLS

Look at the list of 'I can' statements below and think carefully about how confident you are. Use the following code to rate each of the statements. Be honest!

Green – very confident. What is your evidence for this?

Orange – quite confident. What is your target? Be specific.

Red – not confident. What is your target? Be specific.

A self-assessment revision checklist is available on *Kerboodle*

I can...

- Define the term 'human rights' and explain why human rights are important

- Explain different Christian teachings and responses to human rights, with reference to a source of wisdom and authority

- Explain what situation ethics is, and how it relates to human rights

- Explain Christian responses to non-religious arguments about human rights

- Explain Christian teachings about equality, with reference to a source of wisdom and authority

- Give reasons why there is inequality in the world and the problems caused by this

- Describe possible solutions to inequality and the reasons for them

- Explain Christian teachings about religious freedom, with reference to a source of wisdom and authority

- Describe the response of the Church to a multi-faith society

- Describe the benefits and challenges for Christians living in a multi-faith society

- Explain Christian responses to non-religious arguments against aspects of religious freedom

- Explain Christian teachings and responses to prejudice and discrimination and why they are wrong, with reference to a source of wisdom and authority

- Describe the problems caused by prejudice and discrimination

- Explain Christian teachings and responses to racial harmony, with reference to a source of wisdom and authority and situation ethics

- Describe how Christians have worked for racial harmony, with reference to Desmond Tutu

- Explain the benefits for Christians of living in a multi-ethnic society

- Explain Christian teachings and responses towards racial discrimination

- Explain how and why racial discrimination causes problems in society, with reference to a source of wisdom and authority

- Explain Christian teachings and responses to the distribution of wealth and opportunity in the UK and the world

- Explain Christian teachings about social justice, with reference to a source of wisdom and authority

- Describe how the Church works for social justice, with reference to situation ethics

- Explain Christian teachings and responses to the causes of poverty in the UK and in the world, including absolute and relative poverty

- Give Christian teachings about wealth and poverty, including biblical examples, and explain links to virtue ethics.

Exam practice

On these exam practice pages you will see example answers for each of the exam question types: **a**, **b**, **c**, and **d**. You can find out more about these on pages 6–10.

• Question 'a'

*Question **a** is AO1 – this tests your knowledge and understanding.*

> (a) Outline **three** Christian teachings that relate to human rights. (3)

Student response

Do not steal, Do not commit adultery.

Improved student response

The Ten Commandments, particularly do not kill and do not steal, support the human rights to live a full and equal life. Jesus' teaching to love your neighbour as yourself and to love your enemies underpins human rights.

 Over to you! Give yourself three minutes on the clock and have a go at answering this question. Remember, this question type requires you to provide three facts or short ideas: you don't need to explain them or express any opinions.

 WHAT WENT WELL

This student has correctly identified two commandments which support human rights.

 HOW TO IMPROVE

For a high level answer the student should outline three different Christian teachings and make clear the link to human rights. See the 'improved student response' opposite for suggested corrections.

• Question 'b'

*Question **b** is AO1 – this tests your knowledge and understanding.*

> (b) Explain **two** non-religious arguments against aspects of religious freedom. (4)

Student response

Teaching religion in schools is not right as it is argued to 'brainwash' children. Missionaries do not support religious freedom as they force their religion onto others.

Improved student response

Non-religious people may disagree with aspects of religious freedom as they may see the freedoms of others being removed as a result. For example, many people disagree with the teaching of religion in schools as it is argued to indoctrinate children into believing a certain way.

In addition, religious freedom brings missionaries, and many non-religious people believe the evangelistic work of missionaries does not support religious freedom as they force their religious beliefs and teachings onto others.

 Over to you! Give yourself four minutes on the clock and have a go at answering this question. Remember, in order to 'explain' something, you need to **develop** your points. See page 9 for a reminder of how to do this.

 WHAT WENT WELL

This is a low-level response with two basic reasons given. The student does correctly outline some non-religious ideas, however.

 HOW TO IMPROVE

The reasons given are not developed and do not show in detail why non-religious people may not support aspects of religious freedom. For a high level response students should explain the non-religious arguments against aspects of religious freedom. See the 'improved student response' opposite for suggested corrections.

• Question 'c'

*Question **c** is AO1 – this tests your knowledge and understanding.*

> (c) Explain **two** Christian beliefs about prejudice and discrimination. In your answer you must refer to a source of wisdom and authority. (5)

Student response

Christians believe prejudice and discrimination are wrong because everyone is made in God's image and the Bible teaches against it.

WHAT WENT WELL

This is a low level answer which correctly identifies Christian and biblical teaching that prejudice and discrimination is wrong.

Improved student response

Christians believe prejudice and discrimination are wrong because people are taught that everyone is made in God's image: "So God created mankind in his own image, in the image of God he created them; male and female he created them" (Genesis 1:27). Because of this, Christians believe that all people should be treated equally and with respect.

In addition, the Bible teaches against prejudice and discrimination and Christians are taught to follow the teachings of the Bible. Jesus taught people to 'love your neighbour as yourself' and so Christians will actively work to prevent prejudice and discrimination through charity, education and working with other religions.

HOW TO IMPROVE

The student needs to explain, with examples, Christian beliefs about prejudice and discrimination. Has the student included a source of wisdom and authority? See the 'improved student response' opposite for suggested corrections.

 Over to you! Give yourself five minutes on the clock and have a go at answering this question. Remember, you need to write two developed points, one of which needs to be supported by a source of wisdom and authority.

• Question 'd'

*Question **d** is AO2 – this tests your ability to evaluate.*

> (d) 'It is wrong to be wealthy.' Evaluate this statement considering arguments for and against. In your response you should:
> • refer to Christian teachings
> • refer to relevant ethical arguments
> • reach a justified conclusion. (12)

Student response

Wealth is not evenly distributed around the world, and this means that there are people who have to live in absolute poverty while others enjoy a wealthy lifestyle. Even in the UK, the richest 1% has more money than the poorest 55% put together.

Christians believe they have a responsibility to work for social justice and help the poor. However, the Bible teaches that it's wrong to love money, not necessarily wrong to have it: 'Keep your lives free from the love of money' (Hebrews 13: 5). It is possible to be wealthy and have a generous character.

In conclusion, I don't think it's wrong to be wealthy, but I do think it's wrong to be wealthy and have no sense of responsibility to care for the poor. Wealthy Christians should therefore take this responsibility seriously.

Improved student response

Wealth is not evenly distributed around the world, and this means that there are people who have to live in absolute poverty while others enjoy a wealthy lifestyle. Even in the UK, the richest 1% has more money than the poorest 55% put together.

Christians believe they have a responsibility to work for social justice and help the poor, because they are commanded to do so in the Bible: 'Give generously to them...' (Deuteronomy 15: 10). Furthermore, if they do this, it is as if they are helping Jesus himself (Matthew 25: 40). It could be argued therefore that it is wrong to be wealthy if that means ignoring the Christian duty to help the poor.

However, the Bible teaches that it's wrong to love money, not necessarily wrong to have it: 'Keep your lives free from the love of money' (Hebrews 13: 5). This links with virtue ethics, which emphasises character over merely obeying commands. Virtue ethics would claim that it's wrong to be wealthy only if that also reflects a lack of morality. This is shown when Jesus meets the rich young man in Mark 10. He tells the man to sell everything he has and to follow Jesus, but the rich man cannot do this because he loves money. Jesus says 'How hard it is for the rich to enter the kingdom of God!' (10: 23), which means that the love of money is a barrier to people really experiencing God's kingdom.

In conclusion, I don't think it's wrong to be wealthy, but I do think it's wrong to be wealthy and have no sense of responsibility to care for the poor. Wealthy Christians should therefore take this responsibility seriously.

 Over to you! Give yourself 12 minutes on the clock and have a go at answering this question. Remember to refer back to the original statement in your writing when you give different points of view, and make sure you cover each of the bullet points given in the question.

 BUILD YOUR SKILLS

In your exams, you'll need to make sure you use religious terminology correctly. Do you know the meaning of the following important terms for this topic?

human rights   situation ethics   religious freedom   prejudice

equality   social justice   relative poverty   multi-faith

discrimination   virtue ethics   absolute poverty   multi-ethnic

 WHAT WENT WELL

This student understands that they must give two opposing sides of the argument and reach a conclusion. They have referred to a source of wisdom and authority.

 HOW TO IMPROVE

Both sides of the argument lack detailed understanding, and the student has ignored the requirement in the exam question to refer to 'relevant ethical arguments'. See the 'improved student response' opposite for suggested corrections.

Glossary

39 Articles of Religion A historical record of beliefs (or 'doctrines') held by the Church of England

absolute poverty a severe lack of basic human necessities, e.g. food, clean water, sanitation, shelter, education, and health care

adultery a couple having sex even though one (or both) of them is married to someone else.

advent a coming.

Alpha Course a course run by churches and local Christian groups which enables people to find out more about the Christian faith in a relaxed setting.

analogy a comparison between two things that have similarities.

anoint apply oil to a person's head as a sign of holiness and God's approval.

ascension going up into heaven.

atheist someone who does not believe in the existence of God.

atonement the action of restoring a relationship; in Christianity, Jesus' death and resurrection restores the relationship between God and human beings.

baptism the Christian ceremony that welcomes a person into the Christian community.

begotten born of.

benevolence all-good.

charismatic a power given by God, e.g. inspired teaching.

charity giving to those in need.

confirmation the Christian ceremony that accepts a person who formally asks to become a member of the Church.

conservation protecting something from being damaged or destroyed.

convert to change from one set of beliefs to another.

cosmological argument an argument for the existence of God which suggests something must have started the universe.

covenant an agreement between two parties, for example God and humanity.

creationism the belief that the world was created in a literal six days and that Genesis is a scientific/historical account of the beginning of the world.

creed a statement of firmly held beliefs; for example, the Apostles' Creed or the Nicene Creed.

crucifixion being nailed to a cross and left to die.

Day of judgement God assesses a person's life and actions.

denominations the name given to the main groups within the Church.

design argument the argument that God must exist because the universe is so complex, purposeful and beautiful that it had to be created by an intelligent being.

discrimination treating people less favourably because of an irrelevant factor.

ecumenism a movement that tries to bring different Christian denominations closer together.

environment the surroundings in which plants and animals live and on which they depend for life.

epiphany a moment of suddenly revealing something surprising or great.

eschatology an area of Christian theology which is concerned with life after death.

eucharist the ceremony commemorating the Last Supper, involving bread and wine; also called Holy Communion or Mass.

evangelical spreading the Christian message.

evangelism preaching the gospel in order to attract new believers.

false testimony telling lies.

free will having the freedom to choose what to do.

grace undeserved love.

hallucination seeing something that is not really there.

heaven place of eternal paradise where Christians believe they will spend the afterlife.

hell place of punishment and separation from God.

Holy Spirit the Spirit of God, which gives the power to understand and worship.

Holy week the week before Easter.

Humanist a non-religious person who looks to reason and empathy in order to live a meaningful life.

humanity all human beings.

immortal soul a soul that lives on after the death of the body.

incarnation to take on flesh; God becomes a human being.

intercession prayers for those who are suffering.

Jesus Christ the Son of God, who came into the world as a human being.

law guidelines as to how people should behave.

liturgical a set form of worship, usually following agreed words.

local church a meeting place for local believers and the community of believers who gather there.

miracle an amazing or impossible event that brings good, leading to it being thought an act of God.

mission sending individuals or groups to spread the Christian message.

missionary a person who preaches and invites people to convert to the Christian faith.

moral evil suffering caused by humans, such as war.

nativity the birth of someone.

natural evil suffering caused by natural events, such as earthquakes.

near-death experience an experience when someone who later revives is close to death.

non-liturgical a form of worship which is not set.

obligation something that you must do; a responsibility.

omnipotence all-powerful.

outreach an activity to provide services to people in need.

parish a community of local believers within a particular denomination.

Pentecostalism a Protestant movement that puts special emphasis on a direct and personal relationship with God through the Holy Spirit.

persecution the ill-treatment of an individual or group, usually on the grounds of religion, politics or ethnicity.

philosophy the study of truths about life, morals etc.

pilgrim someone who goes on a pilgrimage.

pilgrimage a journey to a religious or holy place.

prayer a way of communicating with God.

prejudice a belief that someone is inferior or superior without having any actual experience of them.

prime mover the first cause of all other things.

prohibition something that is not allowed to happen.

prophecy a message from God in which he communicates his will.

purgatory a place where the souls of the dead are cleansed and prepared for heaven.

racial harmony people from different races and cultures living together amicably in one society.

racism the belief that some races are inferior to others.

reconciliation restoring peace and friendship between individuals or groups.

relative poverty being significantly worse off than the majority of the population.

religious experience an event that a person believes has brought them in direct contact with God.

repentance to say sorry for, and turn away from, any wrongdoing.

resurrection rising from the dead.

revelation when a truth is revealed that was previously hidden.

sacrament an important Christian ceremony.

salvation being saved from sin and the consequences of sin; going to heaven.

Satan 'the adversary'; one of God's angels who rebelled against the rule of God.

sermon a talk or teaching from a church leader.

shrine a holy place.

sin anything that prevents a relationship with God, either because the person does something they shouldn't, or neglects to do something they should.

situation ethics ethical decisions are made according to the specific context of the decision.

Social justice restoring equality and human rights to those in need, especially in relation to unfair distribution of wealth and opportunity.

spiritual gifts gifts given by God to believers, e.g. speaking in 'tongues', a special language.

stewardship looking after something so it can be passed on to the next generation.

Trinity God as one being, in three persons.

universalism the belief that because of the love and mercy of God everyone will go to heaven.

vale of soul-making an environment in which human beings can overcome evil by making good choices.

vigil staying awake at night in order to pray; also the name given to the celebration of a festival on the eve before the festival itself.

violate to break a law or agreement.

virtue ethics an ethical theory that emphasises character and morality above merely obeying rules.

vision seeing or hearing someone or something holy.

worship believers expressing love and respect for, and devotion to, God.

Index

Acknowledgements

We are grateful to the authors and publishers for use of extracts from their titles and in particular for the following:

Scripture quotations taken from the **Holy Bible, New International Version Anglicised** Copyright © 1979, 1984, 2011 Biblica. Used by permission of Hodder & Stoughton Ltd, an Hachette UK company. All rights reserved. 'NIV' is a registered trademark of Biblica UK trademark number 1448790.

Excerpts from **Catechism of the Catholic Church**, http://www.vatican.va/archive/ccc_css/archive/catechism/ccc_toc.htm (Strathfield, NSW: St Pauls, 2000). © Libreria Editrice Vaticana. Reproduced with permission from The Vatican.

Christian Aid: *About Us*, http://www.christianaid.org.uk/aboutus/who/aims/our_aims.aspx (Christian Aid, 2016). Reproduced with permission from Christian Aid.

Church Action on Poverty: *About Us* (Church Action on Poverty, 2016). Reproduced with permission from Church Action on Poverty.

Church Action on Poverty: *It's Time to Close the Gap* (Church Action on Poverty, 2016). Reproduced with permission from Church Action on Poverty.

Church Action on Poverty: *Partnerships* (Church Action on Poverty, 2016). Reproduced with permission from Church Action on Poverty.

St Thomas Aquinas: *Summa Theologica* (Benziger Bros, 1947). Reproduced with permission from The Dominican Council.

G. Kendrick: *Shine, Jesus, Shine*, (Make Way Music, 1987) Graham Kendrick © (1987) Make Way Music. www.grahamkendrick.co.uk. Reproduced with permission from Make Way Music.

The Methodist Church in Britain: *Methodist Conference 2009*, Motion 203 (The Methodist Church in Britain, 2009). Reproduced with permission from The Methodist Church in Britain.

We have made every effort to trace and contact all copyright holders before publication, but if notified of any errors or omissions, the publisher will be happy to rectify these at the earliest opportunity.

The publisher would like to thank the following for permission to use their photographs:

COVER: Jake Lyell / Alamy Stock Photo

p4: Lolostock / Shutterstock; **p8**: Photoonlife / Shutterstock; **p9**: totallypic / Shutterstock; **p10**: Nikolaeva / Shutterstock; **p11**: SH-Vector / Shutterstock; **p12**: Sutichak / Shutterstock; **p13**: Tang Yan Song / Shutterstock; **p14**: Photobank gallery/Shutterstock; **p14**: Eugene Sergeev/Shutterstock; **p17**: The Baptism of Christ, c.1580-88 (oil on canvas), Veronese, (Paolo Caliari) (1528-88) / © Samuel Courtauld Trust, The Courtauld Gallery, London, UK / Bridgeman Images; **p18**: © Jeff Gilbert / Alamy Stock Photo; **p19**: Lisa S./Shutterstock; **p21**: robert_s/ Shutterstock; **p23**: © Gregg Vignal / Alamy Stock Photo; **p23**: Amy Watts; **p24**: © AF archive / Alamy Stock Photo; **p25**: © Paul Rapson / Alamy Stock Photo; **p26**: © Archivart / Alamy Stock Photo; **p27**: Photobank gallery/Shutterstock; **p28**: © AF archive / Alamy Stock Photo; **p28**: Lokibaho/iStock; **p29**: Colin Underhill / Alamy Stock Photo; **p30**: Heritage Image Partnership Ltd / Alamy Stock Photo; **p31**: © Archivart / Alamy Stock Photo; **p32**: Samuel Cohen / Shutterstock; **p33**: Iakov Kalinin/Shutterstock; **p34**: Iulian Dragomir/Shutterstock; **p34**: Steve Skjold/Alamy Stock Photo; **p36**: WitthayaP/Shutterstock; **p36**: ZUMA Press, Inc. / Alamy Stock Photo; **p38**: Jorge Fajl/National Geographic Creative/Corbis; **p39**: Eugene Sergeev/Shutterstock;

p40: © Design Pics Inc / Alamy Stock Photo; **p41**: Michaelpuche/ Shutterstock; **p46**: Adam Radosavljevic / Shutterstock; **p46**: Design Pics Inc / Alamy Stock Photo; **p48**: IanSt8 / Shutterstock; **p49**: mangostock / Shutterstock; **p50**: Peter Barritt / Alamy Stock Photo; **p51**: Lolostock / Shutterstock; **p52**: Granger, NYC. / Alamy Stock Photo; **p52**: epa european pressphoto agency b.v. / Alamy Stock Photo; **p53**: Agencja Fotograficzna Caro / Alamy Stock Photo; **p54**: Mike H / Shutterstock; **p55**: Lebrecht Music and Arts Photo Library / Alamy Stock Photo; **p56**: OLIVIER LABAN-MATTEI/AFP/Getty Images; **p57**: Adam Radosavljevic / Shutterstock; **p58**: VitalyEdush / iStock; **p58**: Mindia Charkseliani / Shutterstock; **p59**: Eddies Images / Shutterstock; **p61**: Design Pics Inc / Alamy Stock Photo; **p62**: KHIN MAUNG WIN/AFP/Getty Images; **p62**: Chronicle / Alamy Stock Photo; **p63**: Alistair Scott / Alamy Stock Photo; **p63**: Zhukov Oleg / Shutterstock; **p64**: RTimages / Shutterstock; **p65**: Darryl Dyck/Bloomberg via Getty Images; **p66**: Calek / Shutterstock; **p67**: 3Dalia / Shutterstock; **p68**: Igor Zh. / Shutterstock; **p69**: Folio Images / Alamy Stock Photo; **p70**: Friedrich Stark / Alamy Stock Photo; **p70**: SpeedKingz / Shutterstock; **p76**: Skim New Media Limited / Alamy Stock Photo; **p76**: Nancy Bauer / Shutterstock; **p78**: Pontino / Alamy Stock Photo; **p79**: Art Directors & TRIP / Alamy Stock Photo; p81: Shutterstock; **p82**: TerryHealy / Getty Images; **p83**: Mkucova / iStock; **p84**: Godong / Alamy Stock Photo; **p85**: Chokniti Khongchum / Shutterstock; **p86**: elenaleonova / Getty Images; **p86**: Granger, NYC. / Alamy Stock Photo; **p87**: Mary Evans Picture Library / Alamy Stock Photo; **p88**: Muammar Awad/Anadolu Agency/Getty Images; **p89**: robertharding / Alamy Stock Photo; **p90**: Barry Lewis / Alamy Stock Photo; **p91**: KAREN MINASYAN/AFP/Getty Images; **p92**: The Resurrection of Christ and the Pious Women at the Sepulchre, 1442 (fresco), Angelico, Fra (Guido di Pietro) (c.1387-1455) / Museo di San Marco dell'Angelico, Florence, Italy / Bridgeman Images; **p93**: Amy Mikler / Alamy Stock Photo; **p94**: Borderlands / Alamy Stock Photo; **p95**: Alpha; **p97**: Peter Noyce GEN / Alamy Stock Photo; **p97**: Jim West / Alamy Stock Photo; **p98**: Vatican Pool/Getty Images; **p99**: epa european pressphoto agency b.v. / Alamy Stock Photo; **p101**: Rana Sajid Hussain/Pacific Press/LightRocket via Getty Images; **p101**: Frances Roberts / Alamy Stock Photo; **p102**: Sam Spickett/ Christian Aid; **p108**: Janine Wiedel Photolibrary / Alamy Stock Photo; **p108**: Dan Vincent / Alamy Stock Photo; **p111**: Photofusion/REX/Shutterstock; **p111**: www.worldvision.org.uk; **p112**: DYLAN MARTINEZ/AFP/Getty Images; **p113**: Nick Harvey/WireImage/Getty Images; **p114**: Dan Kitwood/Getty Images; **p114**: Janine Wiedel Photolibrary / Alamy Stock Photo; **p115**: Max Mumby/Indigo/Getty Images; **p116**: epa european pressphoto agency b.v. / Alamy Stock Photo; **p117**: Franco Origlia/Getty Images; **p118**: Shutterstock; **p119**: mark phillips / Alamy Stock Photo; **p120**: B Christopher / Alamy Stock Photo; **p120**: PETER PARKS/AFP/Getty Images; **p121**: AC Rider / Shutterstock; **p122**: Shutterstock; **p123**: David Turnley/Corbis/VCG via Getty Images; **p123**: Jan Hamman/ Foto24/Gallo Images/Getty Images; **p124**: Central Press/Getty Images; **p124**: Clive Chilvers / Shutterstock; **p125**: Photo Researchers / Alamy Stock Photo; **p126**: Janine Wiedel Photolibrary / Alamy Stock Photo; **p126**: Janine Wiedel Photolibrary / Alamy Stock Photo; **p127**: picture that / Alamy Stock Photo; **p128**: Used by permission of Church Action on Poverty, www.church-poverty.org.uk; **p129**: epa european pressphoto agency b.v. / Alamy Stock Photo; **p130**: Dan Vincent / Alamy Stock Photo; **p130**: JW LTD / Getty Images; **p131**: Jim West / Alamy Stock Photo.